SOUL MASTERY

ALSO BY SONIA CHOQUETTE

Read Life Accurately

The Answer Is Simple . . .
Love Yourself, Live Your Spirit! *

The Answer Is Simple Oracle Cards*

Ask Your Guides*

Ask Your Guides Oracle Cards*

Diary of a Psychic*

The Intuitive Spark*

The Power of Your Spirit*

The Psychic Pathway

The Psychic Pathway to Joy

The Psychic Pathway to New Beginnings

Soul Lessons and Soul Purpose*

Soul Lessons and Soul Purpose Oracle Cards*

The Time Has Come . . .
to Accept Your Intuitive Gifts!*

Traveling at the Speed of Love*

True Balance

Trust Your Vibes at Work, and Let Them Work for You*

Trust Your Vibes Oracle Cards*

Tune In*

Vitamins for the Soul*

Grace Guidance and Gifts*

The Intuitive Spark*

Waking Up in Paris: Overcoming Darkness in the City of Lights*

Walking Home: A Journey from Humbled to Healed*

Your Three Best Superpowers: Meditation, Imagination & Intuition*

Your Heart's Desire

*Available from Hay House
Please visit:

Hay House UK: www.hayhouse.co.uk
Hay House USA: www.hayhouse.com®
Hay House Australia: www.hayhouse.com.au
Hay House India: www.hayhouse.co.in

SOUL MASTERY

22 Lessons to Reinvent Your Life

SONIA CHOQUETTE

HAY HOUSE

Carlsbad, California • New York City
London • Sydney • New Delhi

Published in the United Kingdom by:
Hay House UK Ltd, 1st Floor, Crawford Corner,
91–93 Baker Street, London W1U 6QQ
Tel: +44 (0)20 3927 7290; www.hayhouse.co.uk

Text © Sonia Choquette, 2025

Cover design: Sky High Interactive (Becca/Yoni)
Interior design: Bryn Starr Best

The moral rights of the authors have been asserted.

All rights reserved. No part of this book may be reproduced by any mechanical, photographic or electronic process, or in the form of a phonographic recording; nor may it be stored in a retrieval system, transmitted or otherwise be copied for public or private use, other than for 'fair use' as brief quotations embodied in articles and reviews, without prior written permission of the publisher.

The information given in this book should not be treated as a substitute for professional medical advice; always consult a medical practitioner. Any use of information in this book is at the reader's discretion and risk. Neither the authors nor the publisher can be held responsible for any loss, claim or damage arising out of the use, or misuse, of the suggestions made, the failure to take medical advice or for any material on third-party websites.

A catalogue record for this book is available from the British Library.

Tradepaper ISBN: 978-1-83782-246-1
E-book ISBN: 978-1-4019-7782-5
Audiobook ISBN: 978-1-4019-7783-2

10 9 8 7 6 5 4 3 2 1

This product uses responsibly sourced papers, including recycled materials and materials from other controlled sources. For more information, see www.hayhouse.co.uk

The authorized representative in the EU for product safety and compliance is Penguin Random House Ireland, Morrison Chambers, 32 Nassau Street, Dublin D02 YH68, Ireland. https://eu-contact.penguin.ie

Printed and bound by CPI Group (UK) Ltd, Croydon CR0 4YY

CONTENTS

Preface vii
Introduction xv

PART I: **NEW UNDERSTANDING**
Lesson 1: Your Intention Is Your Power 3
Lesson 2: Your Feelings Are Your Fuel 11
Lesson 3: Your Imagination Drives Your Experience
 into Being 21
Lesson 4: Commitment Is Intention in Action 27
Lesson 5: Your Inner Guidance Is Your Compass 33
Lesson 6: The Loving Universe Is Your Partner 39
Lesson 7: Surrender to Love 45

PART II: **NEW BEHAVIORS**
Lesson 8: Becoming Present 57
Lesson 9: Be Quiet and Listen 63
Lesson 10: All Is in Divine Order 67
Lesson 11: A Gift in Everything 73
Lesson 12: Look Past Appearances 77
Lesson 13: Choose with Love 83
Lesson 14: Endings and Beginnings 89
Lesson 15: Meet Life with Grace 97
Lesson 16: Live in Integrity 105
Lesson 17: Lead Your Life 113
Lesson 18: Free Your Spirit 119
Lesson 19: Live Joyfully 127
Lesson 20: Create Your Life 135
Lesson 21: Shine Your Light 145
Lesson 22: The New You 153

About the Author 167

PREFACE

In 2002, I was invited to teach on a cruise ship sailing along the western coast of Mexico. I was a guest speaker for my publisher, Hay House, and between teaching sessions, I found myself enjoying a wonderful experience, grateful to be allowed to share my work in such a serene and uplifting atmosphere. One evening after dinner, I impulsively went up to the upper deck and meditated under the stars. While sitting quietly, I suddenly became aware of a brand-new group of spirit guides I had not encountered before. While I had been working with spirit guides my entire life, I was unfamiliar with this particular group of guides' unique frequency and energy. They felt direct but loving. My mind went silent as I listened for their energy. But as soon as they appeared, they vanished and the transmission subsided, leaving me wondering if I had imagined it all. Moments later, they reappeared again and, this time, said, *"We are the Emissaries of the Third Ray, second octave of love, and as spokesperson, I am Joachim."*

My heart jumped, and I sat up straight; they now had my full attention. Again silence. After another few minutes, the Emissaries continued, communicating more clearly this time. They shared that the Earth's frequency was shifting, and they were here to teach humans how to navigate this shift gracefully. They further explained that they were a group of light beings, teachers from the fifth dimension who've come to teach humans how to activate their light bodies, and, more specifically, how to use their energy to manifest successfully on the earth plane. The Emissaries intended their instruction to help humanity create lives they desired, but also to positively influence and elevate the frequency of the planet itself to a higher vibration. They explained that they chose me to channel this information into a book called *Soul Lessons and Purpose* because my soul was available as a messenger.

I listened, then agreed because I was a willing messenger for this transmission. Still, I had to get my publisher to get on board for this transmission to be shared. Not surprisingly, Reid Tracy, my publisher and a great support person, said, "Well, if those are your instructions, let's do it." With his blessing, I began writing what the Emissaries dictated to me over the next six months: 22 soul lessons on manifesting in the third dimension. The number 22 did not surprise me. The Emissaries contacted me in the year 2002. That was the first time the number 22 appeared. From my own spiritual and metaphysical in-depth training from when I was 12 years old, I also knew that the number 22 resonated very specifically with how to manifest in the physical plane. Twenty-two is a sacred number reflecting how the physical world manifests through consciousness, emotion, and action. In my studies of Western Kabbalah, the number 22 is considered the path between the divine and the material world. I also knew from my studies of over 22 years (at that time) that it was no coincidence that the first 22 numbers symbolize, reflect, and teach the cosmic principles and pathways behind all manifestation.

In addition to the spiritual importance of the first 22 numbers, the Hebrew alphabet is composed, not coincidentally, of 22 letters, each corresponding to a number that represents a spiritual law. Also, from my extensive metaphysical training with my teachers over many years, I knew there are

Preface

22 archetypes in the major arcana of a tarot deck, a pictorial system on how to manifest according to Western mystery school teachings, Western Kabbalah. This training composed a considerable part of my spiritual education. I knew from these traditions that 22 is a significant and sacred number; it's *the* number for manifestation.

I did channel the Emissaries' instructions back then and shared them in a book called *Soul Lessons and Soul Purpose*. It was released many years ago. So I was surprised when, in 2022, I was once again contacted by Joachim and the Emissaries of the Third Ray, second octave of love, and was asked to write an updated version of the original transmission because the frequency of the Earth, as well as our frequencies as human beings, were undergoing a tremendous transformation and the laws that applied earlier had shifted somewhat. There were still 22 divine laws, they assured me, but these laws have been adjusted to the vibration of the planet right now, because the original 22 laws spoke to humanity manifesting primarily in the third dimension, the dimension of physical density, time, and space, and this limited frequency was now opening to higher vibrations. The Emissaries wanted to assist humans now entering consciousness's higher fourth and fifth dimensions. I understood. The world is profoundly changing, so much so that what we once took for granted, like stable jobs, global health, and a secure environment, is forever gone, and so much we never expected or could have even imagined is showing up, like AI and new currencies. We are not playing in the same world we were used to even 10 short years ago.

This entry of a new Earth vibration began with the pandemic, followed by relentless climate catastrophes and tumultuous Earth and political upheaval. The structures of our present society and culture, most of which manifested out of the old paradigm of the third dimension (primarily that of top-down power and control), are colliding and crumbling before our eyes. When observing on the surface, the world looks like it is in quite an unnerving mess. The Emissaries of the Third Ray, led by Joachim, reassured me that despite appearances, all is evolving, suggesting to me not to judge on appearances alone. *"You are in the midst of a phenomenal evolution and transformation,"* they said, *"and for those who chose to be here now, you are being liberated from the illusions and limitations of time and space and restored to your light bodies. You are evolving into empowered multidimensional light beings at a tremendously rapid pace, and we are here to help."* The Emissaries reappeared to invite me to channel this updated address on how to manifest as light beings vibrating in the fourth and fifth dimensions and beyond, leaving behind our third-dimension consciousness, which was limiting us to the physical world.

For those unfamiliar with the different energetic dimensions, this work addresses the three primary ones affecting our lives now: the third, fourth, and fifth. The first is the third dimension, the physical world around us. When your identity is limited to the third dimension alone, you experience life solely through the eyes and limitations of the ego. And because the ego is a temporary, insecure entity, its distorted perceptions leave you feeling threatened and alone. You become the victim of your false perceptions and powerlessness because, from that disconnect, you can't sense or experience how loved, supported, and connected you are to the universe. Fortunately, living exclusively in the third-dimension frequency is giving way to higher states of consciousness, and humans are spontaneously experiencing higher frequencies and dimensions beyond our physical bodies, raising our consciousness more and more. We are being vibrationally lifted out of the third dimension and are entering the fourth and fifth dimensions of existence.

Entering these higher states of consciousness, the Emissaries explained, is awakening our realization that we are divine light beings. When entering these dimensions, we become aware that we are not merely physical, ego-based limited beings but spirit-embodied light beings, limited only by our imaginations. This revelation frees us from the restrictions of time and space. According to the Emissaries, humans elected to be here on Earth to learn to use their sacred energy and power to create and manifest the lives as they wished them to unfold. The Emissaries pointed out that when creating solely from the third dimension of consciousness, we become trapped by time and space, giving us the impression that matter is separate from us and not something we influence with our thinking and feeling. This misperception is causing so much damage to ourselves and the planet that the Emissaries have returned to assist in accelerating our ascension to higher frequencies of consciousness: Entering these higher dimensions of consciousness frees our fear and restores our divine power of unlimited creativity. When creating from these higher dimensions, we remove the illusions and limitations that cause us to struggle and suffer, fear life, and hurt ourselves and others.

The fourth and fifth dimensions are not physical places. They are higher states of mind fueled by unconditional love. In these higher domains of energy, we recognize and experience ourselves as pure, eternal light. We become one with the universe and experience ourselves as unlimited, unconditional love.

To help clarify the difference in energetic and vibrational dimensions, the Emissaries suggest imagining each dimension as a specific frequency or energetic and vibrational bandwidth, much like a radio transmission. The third dimension can be equated with the energetic bandwidth of an AM radio broadcast, which, if you listen to this frequency, you can agree is comprised of mostly talk and bantered opinion, much of which is combative, can be polarizing, and is usually fear-based. The fourth dimension can then be equated with a higher-end, somewhat stronger FM radio transmission. This bandwidth tends to be populated with more inspired communication and a great deal of beautiful music. An FM radio broadcast is generally soothing, sophisticated, elevated, uplifting, and pleasant. In the fourth dimension, our energy is primarily broadcast through thoughts, emotions, and imaginings.

Continuing to elevate our consciousness, we enter the fifth dimension, the frequency of unconditional love. When we enter this dimension of consciousness, our egos become quiet, and we tune in to our hearts, where we discover pure love. The fifth dimension can be compared to satellite transmission, expanding our capability to receive and send out loving energy at an exponentially higher and faster rate. When attuned to the fifth dimension, we recognize we are light beings and reclaim our divine nature. In the fifth dimension, the ego recedes, and our light body takes over. Once we embody our light, we become aware of other light beings, both fellow humans and beings in these higher dimensions such as angels, spirit guides, ancestors, and more. When attuned to the fifth dimension, we also activate our innate intuitive abilities. These include clairvoyance, or clear viewing, or the ability to see past the illusions of our ego fears, past the biases of our intellect, and into the true nature of life. We activate the inner sense of clairaudience, listening to life with our entire bodies and not our physical ears alone. Moreover, we cease to focus on external sound and tune in to energy and vibration, which inform and guide us toward all that is congruent with our spirit and away from what is incongruent with our best and highest good. We also activate clairsentience, sensing the presence of subtle energy and assistance from our angels, spirit guides, helpers, and healing teams in spirit, Divine Creator, and more. The Emissaries serve as our guide into these higher dimensions so we can express our divine nature.

I was eager to join the Emissaries and was ready to record their transmission and share it. But before I fully committed to Joachim, I stopped short and asked, "Are the Emissaries here to tell us to follow *rules*? Because knowing humans (me included), we tend to want to break the rules rather than follow them."

With this, they chuckled. *"Yes, we acknowledge the ego doesn't like rules because the ego wants to be in control, but these are not rules to submit to. We share the divine laws that operate throughout the universe. They are impersonal. Much like understanding how a computer system operates will allow you to gain the most of its use, knowing how the divine system works will allow you to reap its benefits and blessings.*

"If you know how you, as a light being, are designed to create and work with the laws of the universe, you avoid obstacles, save energy, and experience unlimited and predictable outcomes. This is the reason for our transmission. To help you recognize yourselves as multidimensional light beings with unlimited power to create and to show you how to make this easy."

What follows is the transmission from Joachim and the Emissaries of the Third Ray, second octave of love. Everything written in italics is their direct transmission. Following, in regular font, I share my own experiences, both as a teacher and a student, in understanding these laws and accepting and applying them. Together, we hope this guide will assist you in entering the higher dimensions and reclaiming your innate divine power and peace. If you're ready (and I believe you are because you've been drawn to this transmission in the first place), let us begin.

INTRODUCTION

Welcome. I am Joachim, and we are the Emissaries of the Third Ray, second octave of love. We are so honored to have your attention and are at your service in elevating and empowering your divine nature. We come before you to share the 22 divine laws of manifestation that reign throughout the universe and hope to enhance your understanding of these laws, including how to apply them while in Earth's creation school. As you know, the Earth's vibration and frequency are rapidly changing, and your planet is undergoing a powerful shift. Have no fear. The fact that you are here affirms that you have volunteered to be part of this great shift. These are the most exciting of times, and we hope to help you take great advantage of this.

In the following transmission, we wish to reintroduce the 22 sacred divine laws of manifestation and mastery, one at a time, and explain how to use them. We wish to guide your energy to a higher, more empowering vibration. Some of these laws may be familiar, as many already recognize your divine nature. Yet, for some, encountering this transmission and these laws may be new and challenging to accept. In this case, we ask that you consider these 22 divine laws and put them into practice before deciding on their merit. Apply each divine law, one at a time, then draw your conclusions. We aim to assist you in the highest way by activating your light body and awakening your divine powers and creative *consciousness as light beings. Our highest wish is to help you relax and flow in Earth's creation school most joyfully.*

◆ ◆ ◆

As the Emissaries stated, there are 22 divine laws of soul mastery. The Emissaries present these 22 laws as invitations to activate your light body and reclaim your divine nature. The best way to approach these transmissions is to study each law, one at a time, reflecting on whether or not the law is familiar to you, and then apply this divine law fully in creating your life.

The Emissaries also point out that we pass through four stages of learning: student, apprentice, journeyman, and master. In stage one, student, we are introduced to the divine law, perhaps through reading a book or hearing it from someone, usually a friend, intent on growing spiritually for the first time. The next stage is "apprentice." In this stage of learning, we seek a teacher or teachers to demonstrate how to best apply these laws in a way that appeals to us. We follow the lead and model the teacher or mentor until we are deeply familiar with the law and how to apply it. The third stage of learning is called "journeyman." In this stage, we have learned the laws and now enter a phase where we come to own them through our own life experiences. Following these first three stages, we then enter the mastery stage. In the mastery stage, we continue to grow by becoming teachers or role models to our fellow humans. In this way, all beings are students, apprentices, journeymen, and masters, simultaneously, depending on which laws we have learned and at what stage we are in on that learning curve.

To help us better understand the application of the laws, the Emissaries have asked me to contribute my experiences as a teacher and a student, so I share examples of these laws in action. To help integrate the laws, the Emissaries may suggest simple adjustments to your outlook or daily practices to move you along the four stages gracefully. Passing through these four stages of learning is natural and leaves us feeling calmer, more creative, empowered, secure, connected, and satisfied. Our outer world of relationships, health, and abundance improves as well when we move from stage to stage. The more connected we are to our light bodies, the more our hearts open, and with open hearts, the more naturally we resonate with the frequency of the fifth dimension of unconditional love or higher. This is our original frequency and our highest resonant vibration.

The best way to approach this transmission is to familiarize yourself with each law and identify at which stage you are in on the learning curve. While the laws themselves are consecutive and follow a natural order, one laying the foundation for the next, this is not how humans generally have come to learn them. We humans hopscotch through the laws, quickly mastering some and struggling with others, which creates gaps in the flow and frustration in your life. Hopefully, this transmission will highlight your blind spots and fill in the gaps by identifying each law and demonstrating various stages of learning, thus showing how to build a beautiful life learning one law and accepting one invitation at a time.

Again, the first stage is "student." When in the student stage, the law will feel relatively new. You may even find it hard to accept or believe. If this is the case, the Emissaries invite you to suspend your judgment and replace it with curiosity. Follow the law and see what happens. You'll usually have evidence of its merit quickly.

If you have already been introduced to a particular law, perhaps even have begun to integrate it into your consciousness but haven't yet found your confidence, you have entered the apprentice stage of learning. At this stage, you learn best by observing others applying the law. This can be a friend, a partner, a teacher, or even the author of a book or blog. Consciously seek those who follow this law easily and observe their outcomes. When entering the apprentice stage, you activate your light body, open your heart, expand your mind, and make yourself more available to the universe. Once a law is comfortably understood and practiced enough at the apprentice level, you move to the next stage, journeyman.

You become a journeyman when you automatically respect and follow the divine laws without thinking or hesitation. They are now a part of how you feel and act naturally. Consciously following a divine law is no longer something you hesitate to do. Instead, you naturally respect the law and put it to work for you. The journeyman stage is "learning by doing." It is a most exciting and rewarding period, and the Emissaries invite you to trust your divine nature to enjoy your process as you take over at this stage.

Remember when, as a child, you learned to ride a bike? In the student and apprentice stages, you observed the process and then, most likely, rode the bike with training wheels. In the journeyman stage, the training wheels come off, and you discover your balance through practice, knowing full well you may fall, but you are no longer afraid of pain. In the journeyman stage, your desire to see how far you can go is greater than holding yourself back out of fear of hurting yourself.

Eventually, with enough practice, you acquire confidence. At this point, you leave the journeyman stage and enter mastery. In this stage, you have fully integrated that divine law into your consciousness, and it becomes your way of being. You find yourself living with the ease and flow of your light body. You easily recognize which of the 22 divine laws you have mastered by how empowered and successful you are in this or that aspect of your life. When mastering divine laws, intentions manifest so quickly you cannot imagine any other way of being. Too many beautiful experiences unfold at this stage—physically, emotionally, and mentally—to question or challenge the laws. Having mastered a divine law, the inevitable result is peace of mind, joy, ease, and abundance. At the master stage, you leave the learning curve and become a teacher to those around you. In this way, every soul on Earth is simultaneously a student apprentice, journeyman, and master.

When consistently applying the 22 laws of divine mastery, we ultimately learn that we are light beings, divinely connected, and all one. The Emissaries are here to assist in this revelation. Accept their invitation. Learn these laws. Trust your experience as you go. Be patient with your transformation. It's frightening for the ego to let go of control. It will fight on many occasions. Expect this and have a sense of humor and fun. Higher vibrational living does not require a struggle. Struggling is an element and a practice of the third dimension. Examine these laws with curiosity, humor, and receptivity, and know you will receive all the support you need, without a fight.

PART I

NEW UNDERSTANDING

LESSON 1

YOUR INTENTION IS YOUR POWER

Welcome, dear one. We are delighted to have your attention as we escort you into the power, beauty, love, and expression of your divine light being. We invite you to consider, accept, and embody that you are a divine being made of light. Even though you have experienced many limitations in your life so far, your light body is now being activated, and with that, your true nature and power are being restored. We repeat, you are a divine, immortal, holy, and sacred light being—a powerful co-creator of the loving universe. When you recognize and accept this, your experiences in life will ease dramatically, lifting you out of the limitations of the darkened third dimension and into the higher frequencies of your light body residing in the fourth and fifth dimensions of consciousness. Peace will return, abundance will flow, and joy will be your natural state.

The ego doesn't recognize your divine nature. It is dense, wounded, and fearful. Your ego is a temporary entity, constructed in the limited third dimension, devoid of light, and which you are now being encouraged to move beyond. Breathe into this awakening of your true light being self rather than fight, resist, or struggle against it. Open your mind and heart, and breathe back into the expanded beingness of who you are: a pure, light, divine being.

To help you embrace your divine nature, recognize that not everything in your life has been painful, although there are moments and even extended periods when you felt otherwise. Many of your life experiences, or your life's creations, have brought great joy and satisfaction. You created these successes with your divine nature. No matter what you created, however simple or seemingly insignificant, all joyful experiences prove that you are indeed a beautiful, divine co-creator with the universe. Even though your egoic mind likes to diminish or ignore your successes, it cannot deny that you are a creator. Pause now to appreciate your tremendous creative power by reflecting on your past creations. They could be as simple as creating a bicycle that gives you joy when riding or creating a beautiful dinner that gives you pleasure to enjoy and share with others. It could be making a lovely garden that is uplifting to behold, writing a poem, composing a piece of music, or taking an enchanting photograph to move the heart. These are all beautiful and powerful creations.

Take a breath now, in through the nose, dear one, and as you exhale, feel the life force flowing through you, giving your heart the power to beat. Notice how the life force channeled through your breath energizes every part of your magnificent body. As you breathe, recognize that you are so much more than your ego allows you to believe. Your light body is waking up. Let it rise. Let it expand with a deep inhale and flow through you with a heart-centering sigh.

We invite you to do this now. Breathing in, opening your jaw, sighing loudly, and sliding your consciousness into your heart. Feel your spirit expanding in all directions as you do this. Allow it to extend as far as possible. Relax and enjoy. You have just stepped into your light body.

The first divine law of creative mastery, and your first invitation, is to vibrate into this higher dimension and expression of you by allowing your light energy to flow into your intentions. Intention, infused with light, is the beginning of your manifesting power.

Your light-infused intention activates your creative process. Such intention initiates every experience you desire. And yes, we can hear your egoic mind refuting this. "It was never my intention to suffer. It was never my intention to be alone. It was never my intention to struggle." To that, we agree. It was not your conscious intention to create any painful experience. Yet your intentions operate on far more than a conscious level. Many, if not most, intentions broadcast just below the conscious level. Therefore, to raise your vibration to a higher dimension and create more desirable outcomes, it is necessary to be mindful of your unconscious intentions and infuse them with light.

Begin to embrace this law now by noticing where you place your attention. If your attention is consumed by the chaos and fear of the darkened third dimension, it prevents you from keeping the light-filled consciousness needed to manifest. When this happens, rather than being in charge of your intentions, the darkened third dimension dictates what is possible. If mesmerized and hypnotized by the chaos of the third dimension, it is easy to believe that nothing good is possible and your intentions mean nothing. This is because the universe mirrors what you focus on back to you, and if the focus is dark and fearful, what is mirrored back will be so as well. Attention focused on the third dimension blocks the light. When this occurs, you no longer have the light needed to fuel your intention. Joining the 3D chorus of those who say the world is beyond repair, you start channeling your creative energy into these collective dark intentions, contributing to the very conditions you want to escape.

Now, dear one, take a deep breath and ask yourself, "Am I prepared to recognize the power of my intention and reclaim my light? Am I willing to take charge of my focus and attention?" Make this easier by acknowledging your past successfully manifested intentions. They affirm your power to create. Perhaps you intended to attend a particular school, for example, and successfully enrolled. Maybe you intended to travel and have now visited many places far and wide. Perhaps you intended to manifest a safe and secure home, one in which you now, quite peacefully, reside. Every present condition in your life mirrors your intentions, from the clothing you wear to the words you say, to how you interact with others, how you show preferences, and even how you express your style. These are all reflections of your intention made manifest.

Intention infused with light is the greatest. Accepting and using this law is one of the most life-transformative advancements you can make. Intention made with your light body engages your true self, divine light being, and powerful co-creator. Your light-infused intention is a powerful force. With awareness, focus, and attention, you release this enormous divine power within. Pause and reflect. Ask yourself, "Do I recognize and own my light and use my power of intention? Do I presently have focused intentions, and if yes, what are they? Is it my intention to suffer? Is it my intention to be angry or fight? Or to be peaceful and secure? Are my intentions in focus darkened and somber, filled with fear and struggle, or are they joyful, light-filled expectations?"

Dear one, your power of intention has worked for you all along. You use this power exceptionally well in the third dimension. Only it isn't called intention. It is called fear. If we were to ask you today what you have feared and what fears have manifested, we are confident you could name many fears very quickly, and whether or not they have manifested outwardly, you've experienced and suffered them all in your mind.

Fear is the leading portal through which most humans focus their intentions. Fear-based, 3D focus is dark, heavy, weakening, and intimidating. It blocks the light and robs you of joy. It is time to liberate yourself from such a somber, deadening experience. Today, we invite you to cease this tendency or habit of channeling intention through fear and consciously create with your powerful light body instead. Take your focus off fear for a moment and direct your curiosity toward light-filled, joyful intentions. This activates *a higher frequency by concentrating on love over fear. This simple shift is all you need to activate your light body and enter a higher dimension of yourself. Light is either filled and expressed from the fifth dimension or darkened and expressed from the third dimension. Once an intention is set and released, the divine laws of the universe must fulfill it.*

Activate your divine power of intention by identifying one small intention that is important to you now. Begin slowly, internally, to sense the light and joy this will bring. This practice quickly lifts you out of the third dimension and recalibrates your vibration into the fourth and up to the fifth dimension, where manifestation becomes easy. Do not overthink. Let yourself feel the lightness of your heart with the fulfillment of this intention. Reinforce this frequency by focusing on the light-filled intention daily, if only for a few minutes. That is quite enough. Let this lightness of being flow through you. Continue this light-filled practice until it becomes second nature.

As we close for today, we remind you that you are a divine, light-filled being. Accept this and be curious about how to exercise your light and power through your intentions. Life will mirror your efforts. Enjoy the process. I am Joachim. We are the Emissaries of the Third Ray, the second octave of love, at your service.

Listening to the Emissaries, I fully recognize the power of intention. I've observed this over and over again, both with my clients and myself. We do create what we intend. I first learned this law from my mother when I was very young. She had formidable power of intention. She's passed into spirit now, but when she was alive, she was fearless.

My mother became a prisoner of war when she was a child. Caught in the chaos of World War II, she lost contact with her family, got rheumatic fever, and lost her hearing;

met and married my father, a liberating American soldier, when she was only 15; and ended up in America not speaking the language; all of this only made her more focused and intentional. Everything my mom intended, she manifested. She never considered that what she intended would be impossible to create. When I was in middle school and was around 10 years old, she announced her intention to become a photographer. My father, a salesman who sold farm equipment, smiled and shook his head, and gave her little encouragement or support. This empowered her all the more. She frequently said to anyone listening, "Mark my words, I will succeed." She then promptly enrolled in a photography correspondence course.

Next, she insisted my father build her a photography studio in the basement of our home, which was already bursting at the seams with the stuff of seven children and two grandparents who lived there. It didn't matter. She was unstoppable. She learned how to use the camera and develop and print photographs. Despite the family's limited budget, she managed to get the equipment she needed to open her business doors within a year. When she needed help, she asked each of her children, me included, to be her assistant, whether photographing a wedding or developing the photographs later. Her intention wasn't a wish, fantasy, or daydream. It was a power. She was so determined that nobody dared question whether it would happen—it did. She was so successful that within three years, not only did she teach herself photography and open a professional studio in the basement of our tiny home, but she also won national awards for beautiful works.

Watching her succeed against all odds, I witnessed firsthand the power of intention. It is a miraculous force that goes way beyond wishful thinking. I can attest to how important it is to listen and believe the Emissaries, drawing from my own experiences with this law. Intention, which arises from the heart, the kind my mom had, is an unstoppable power. But it's not an ego power. It is the power of your spirit, of your fourth- and fifth-dimension self.

When clients share their intentions, I can immediately tell if they will succeed in manifesting them by assessing their power. When you engage your power of intention, your energy *feels* powerful. This energetic activation, originating in the solar plexus and merging with the heart, infuses your aura with light. It's like turning a light on in a dark room. When you are light filled you command attention. The Emissaries are inviting us to reactivate this innate power, this unstoppable force. They remind us that we volunteered to be here at this time. We signed up for creation school. We didn't come here to get pushed around like pinballs in the pinball machine of chaos that dominates the third dimension. We came here to become masterful and magnificent creators. This begins with awakening your power of intention and fearlessly choosing to manifest your goals, one intention at a time.

It's time to consider: What would you love to experience? So much that you'll put your unwavering focus into it? That's what this law requires. Nothing less. Reclaim your power of intention. Own it. Wake up to it, apply it, direct it with 100 percent commitment. When your intention is light filled and unwavering, you attract the power of the universe to help you. This is the first law of divine mastery and your first invitation.

LESSON 2

YOUR FEELINGS ARE YOUR FUEL

Welcome, dear one. I am Joachim, and we are the Emissaries of the Third Ray, second octave of love; we are so honored to have your attention today as we resume. The second law of divine mastery is that your emotions, or "energy in motion," fuel your intentions and accelerate their realization.

Breathe and become aware of your emotions now. Start by reflecting on how you feel about yourself. Notice how your emotions affect your physical body, self-esteem, relationships, and success in the world. Your emotions dictate your experiences. They may be light, joyful, and expansive, or heavy, draining, and depleting. Either way, your experiences mirror them back to you. Accepting this, how do you feel about your life thus far? Does your life mirror these present feelings? Some of you may not find these easy questions to answer. You may have had your feelings controlled or shut down by others or become disconnected from them, robbing you of the energy and insight they offer. No matter how your feelings have been managed in the past, it is time to reconnect to them now and engage their power. Examine your feelings more deeply. Do your feelings support who you are and who you intend to become? Or do they undermine you or leave you in self-doubt? Do your feelings uplift and celebrate you, or do they diminish you, leaving you demoralized and depressed? Your feelings reveal how your energy is directed, either for or against you. To master creativity, it is important to master your feelings and direct them to work in your favor and toward the manifestation of all you desire.

Begin by cleansing your emotional body with vibrations of love and light. This liberates you from any heaviness and despair caused by stagnant, lingering, or past feelings. Heavy feelings are likely trapped from the past. Some of these feelings may not even be your own, more often being absorbed energy from those around you. No matter their origin, feelings are meant to flow, not remain trapped and stuck, repressed, or denied. Feelings fuel creation, but only if they flow freely. Heavy feelings arrest the creative process. It's necessary to clear this dense energy and fuel your intentions with feelings of confidence, positive conviction, and expectation of intentions fulfilled, and expansive gratitude for blessings in advance of their material appearance instead. This is divine law.

How do you liberate and release heavy feelings? First, by listening to what they are communicating. Anger, for example, expresses a need or desire for respect, boundaries, more sovereignty, and protection. Sorrow communicates loss and the need to grieve. Fear communicates a lack of love and connection. Heavier feelings indicate a need for more self-awareness, self-love, and self-care.

All emotions are messengers and serve a purpose. Yet a feeling of joy is the preferred fuel for manifestation. The more joy you feel, the more magnetic and creative power you possess. Joy is a magnet that pulls your desired intentions quickly toward you. Feelings of joy accelerate manifesting intentions. Filling, or fueling, yourself with light, uplifting feelings cleanses and releases heavy emotions and elevates you to the higher frequencies of the fourth and fifth dimensions. This is where all abundance originates.

Emotions offer important feedback and reflect whether you are in energetic alignment with your light being. No feeling or emotion is bad. Yet feelings that leave you with a sense of peace, calm, and expansion free the restrictions of the third dimension and deliver you into the expansive flow of the higher fourth and fifth dimensions.

Listen carefully to your feelings and follow their clues. Cleanse and release feelings from the past as quickly and as often as possible so present feelings can guide you in the moment. Honor your feelings and turn away from, or reject, anything or anyone that leaves you feeling powerless or small. Walk away from energies that steal your joy, discourage your optimism, or darken your light. Use discernment, attention, honesty, and self-love to guide you. A darkened emotion is a sign to change your behavior, focus, or direction. Its presence indicates you are on the wrong path. Your feelings are working to redirect you. Lighter, happier, more expansive feelings lead you to the fourth and fifth dimensions. They strengthen your light body and enhance your creative power. Prioritize such light-infusing feelings and seek them out.

Once again, focus on your feelings right now. Invoke feelings that uplift you, that make you smile or laugh, that open your heart, that delight you, that reassure you. Call forward these feelings, and your intentions will follow.

Another way to quickly elevate your feelings is to listen to music. Music releases stagnant emotional energy and ushers in fresh, optimistic, and expansive energy. The kind of energy that propels your intentions forward. The happier music leaves you feeling, the more empowered to create and manifest you will be. Cleanse your emotional body of stagnant energy with beautiful music, and observe how quickly your life transforms. Do not be subservient to your feelings. Instead, consciously choose the feelings you want to have and leave behind the ones that you don't.

Next, become aware of how thoughts influence your feelings. Notice how your feelings follow your thoughts. What are you thinking now? Feelings mirror self-talk. When you speak to yourself with loving kindness and positive affirmation, your feelings magnetize experiences that will bring more of the same. Negative self-talk and self-condemnation poison your energy body, yet, in the same vein, will attract more poisonous experiences to you. Pause and reflect on how your words influence your feelings. What are you telling yourself now? Your feelings mirror and support your beliefs. If you genuinely intend to be a joyful creator, believe this intention. If you believe it, the outcome is assured. If your feelings conflict with your intentions, reexamine the intention itself. What you feel reveals what you believe. When intention, belief, and feeling align, outcomes are guaranteed.

Emotions can feel wild and uncontrollable. They're not meant to control you. They are intended only to inform you and guide your experience. Take charge of your emotions. Listen to them, and release those that do not support you today. This will quickly activate your light body and concentrate your creative power. Observe your feelings daily, including the tone and vibration they broadcast, to harness this power. Emotions act as a beacon to the universe calling in what you feel.

To release past, stagnant, heavy, negative feeling, breathe and intend to release. Breathe in and release. With each breath, scan your body, filling up with light and life force. With each exhale, empty stagnant energies that no longer serve you, leaving more inner space and power in the moment. Release heavy emotions. Let them go. They have served their purpose. They communicated important information at the time of past experiences. They are no longer valuable and hold you back. When flowing freely, emotions are powerful fuel. When stagnant, they become dangerously toxic. Take charge of your feelings rather than allow your feelings to control you.

Be curious about your feelings. Ask, "What will help me feel more empowered? What will leave me feeling joyful? What lightens me up?" Your ego may resist your intention to feel good. The ego is most comfortable in conflict and pain. Be prepared to override ego resistance. For example, your ego may say, "I don't want to listen to music; I don't feel like contemplating beauty. I don't feel like letting go of the past." Ignore, or better yet, smile or laugh at such *resistance. This is the egoic body clinging to the third dimension with its dense victim energy and resisting change. Your intention is more powerful than your habit. Override it.*

Consciously choose behaviors that leave you feeling lighter and more joyful as well. Use a sense of wonder to elevate your feelings. For example, wonder: How would it feel to be at peace right now? How would it feel to place our attention on something beautiful? How would it feel to be free of the past? Not to deny less optimistic feelings, just not to be controlled by them. Reconnect, reclaim, reinvent your life with the fuel of your beautiful feeling body. Breathe your heart open and be interested in feeling more joy, beauty, and strength. Feeling is fuel and takes you where it is focused. This is the divine law. I am Joachim. We are the Emissaries of the Third Ray, second octave of love.

♦ ♦ ♦

As I contemplated this message from the Emissaries, I recognized how dense, negative feelings affect us, much like being buried under a mound of internal garbage, stifling our spontaneity and sabotaging our intentions. Listening to the Emissaries, I couldn't help but call to mind a client, Diane, with whom I had been working for some time. She desired, more than anything, to get pregnant and have a child. At 37 years old, however, she had been unable to conceive despite having tried for over three years, both naturally and with IVF. Though her intention was clear, her emotions were dark and misaligned. She felt angry with herself that she had waited too long to conceive, furious that she didn't take better care of herself, and frustrated that conception didn't occur naturally. On top of that, she was resentful that she had to go through all these steps—only to be disappointed month after month. Her intentions and her feelings were at war.

Diane's feelings were understandably conflicted and negative. It was difficult for them not to be. Her futile efforts consumed her in every way: physically, emotionally, and financially. I tried to help her realign her feelings with her intention by suggesting she focus on any beautiful and joyful experience. "Can you call to mind even one?" "No," she snapped. "I'm so angry that I can't." I then suggested that she redirect her negative feelings by engaging her intuition. "I know your fear of never succeeding, but what does your inner guidance tell you?" I asked. "That's the crazy thing," she responded immediately. "It tells me I will be a mother and to be patient." "Then, that is what you must do," I responded. "Align your feelings with your inner guidance and stop forcing things for now. Listen to music, watch entertaining shows, and take up a hobby to redirect your mind toward a more creative effort so your emotions can calm down. Take your attention off feeling so defeated. Let your inner guidance direct you for now and reset." I tried to convey to Diane that our emotions influence our outcomes while being sensitive to her sense of loss at the same time. "When our feelings fight our intentions," I said, "doing anything creative can help turn this dead-ended impasse around." It has for me. Years ago, when I first got divorced, I was shattered to pieces, and couldn't seem to pull my feeling body up to any kind of higher frequency, rather than continue to struggle, I signed up for piano and singing lessons three times a week. For those three hours a week, my mind, heart, and feelings were a million miles away from my sorrow and grief. I was actually having fun. Within three months, I experienced long periods of each day free from heavy emotions and more centered in the moment. Desiring a profound life change in my life and wanting to be freed from the sand trap my shattered ego had fallen into, I was surprised when my daughter suggested that she and I move to Paris. How fun is that idea? The few hours of fun I created with my music lessons opened the door for the universe to deliver a beautiful invitation to make a profound life change with this gorgeous inspiration.

Your Feelings Are Your Fuel

I then recalled another client, Ellen, with whom I had spoken months ago. She shared an incredible story about the power and fuel of emotion with me. When she was 40 and newly divorced, she found herself unexpectedly pregnant with a third child, the father being a relative stranger. Shortly after that, she was in a serious bicycle accident that injured her tailbone and damaged her spine. For unknown medical reasons, Ellen's injuries made it impossible for her to walk. After visiting countless doctors to no avail for over 12 years following the birth of her daughter, her traditional bevy of doctors threw their hands in the air and told Ellen they couldn't help her any further, leaving her in agony and demoralized beyond belief.

Then one day, Ellen had had enough. She decided, *"I'm tired of feeling like this. I'm tired of being limited, needy, frustrated, and down on myself. I intend to heal. I want to feel whole again. I don't know how. I don't even know if it's possible, but it's what I want."* Determined, the following year, Ellen resumed her search for healing. This time, she looked to alternative doctors for answers. She traveled to innovative places and holistic healing centers and even underwent stem cell therapy. By the end of the year, she took her first steps in over a decade. With extensive physical therapy and continued emotional support, Ellen is now out of her wheelchair for good.

When we spoke, I asked her, in awe, "What changed, Ellen? How do you think this happened?" She answered quickly, "I changed my feelings about myself and my life. When I first learned I was pregnant so late in life, I was shocked. I felt fearful and overwhelmed. I mostly felt incapable of assuming this responsibility on my own. I didn't want to. Honestly, when I had that accident, I was almost relieved not to be expected to be so responsible. Eventually, though, I tired of those feelings. I wanted to feel strong again and physically and metaphorically stand on my two feet again. I was ready. Call me a late bloomer, but better late than never. I love the freedom I'm now creating for myself. My recovery so empowered me that I feel invincible; I'm deeply grateful for the help of all the healers and doctors along the way, but I'm convinced my change of feeling is what restored my ability to walk."

And here's another interesting thing. Ellen's intense feelings of empowerment activated the same feeling in me, by just listening to her. After we spoke, I became deeply inspired to tackle my own limitations. And I did. Her invincible feeling and force drift captured my feelings, demonstrating how we absorb others' energies, for good or bad. Since then, I've noticed how much we constantly exchange feelings with others. It happens just as quickly as we exchange thoughts. The second law is clear. Our feelings either empower or sabotage our intentions. If we fuel our intentions with negative feelings, they go nowhere. If we fuel them with positive expectations and advance gratitude, they show up at our front door.

Even though our intentions require emotional fuel to manifest successfully, sadly, for far too many of us, feelings are deadened, ambivalent, or work against our intentions. We don't have to be held back by that, however. We can use our imaginations to jump-start our feelings into flow. One of my favorite ways to do this is, "Fake it till you make it." People with clear intentions feel very strongly that they will succeed. They do not consider failure as an option. They almost approach creating like a game they refuse to lose. Ellen passionately wanted to walk again and was willing to do all she had to do to get there. This is valuable insight. If you approach manifesting your intentions with feelings of love and devotion, they appear twice as fast. When you have fun, your feelings expand, rise, and flow fully. They become contagious and attract all kinds of unexpected support. When you are having fun, your light body becomes activated, and your spirit takes over. The ego steps aside, and your divine power steps in.

This reminds me of another student, Tanya, who attended one of my workshops years ago. Tanya had been so deeply wounded from a toxic childhood that she could barely open her mouth and speak out while she was there. To her horror, I was guided to invite her on stage one afternoon. She was paralyzed with fear once up there. Suddenly, my intuition directed me to put on music, and I chose a silly song with shock lyrics. It surprised Tanya so much that her eyes popped open, and she laughed out loud. In that moment, Tanya let go of all those old feelings she had been carrying for so long. In one instant, she changed before our eyes. Her energy shifted from dense, depressed, and frightened to suddenly confident. She even began to dance. It was as if she had popped out of a cocoon. Tanya was so surprised by the lyrics and their effect on her that it distracted her from the heavy feelings controlling her all these years. She kept laughing, and as she did, she spontaneously entered the fifth dimension. And just like that, she was free. Tanya left a liberated person. She was now in her light body and determined not to look back. Tanya wrote to me a year later, saying she never did return to her old, fearful self. Her feelings fueled newfound joy. That was her intention when she signed up for the class. She succeeded.

The Emissaries are not suggesting we deny our feelings. They're inviting us to release them once they are felt. Moreover, they do invite us to seek positive feelings and make choices that invite such feelings in. In all cases, allow your emotions to be registered, honored, listened to, and then released. They are designed to inform you and move on, not stick around. Learn from your emotions and then let them go. That is the path to mastering divine law number two.

LESSON 3

YOUR IMAGINATION DRIVES YOUR EXPERIENCE INTO BEING

Dear one, are you beginning to feel the joy of becoming a light being, entering a higher vibration, and creating a new Earth? Is it not exciting? Can you not help but be curious about this expanded reality? Can you feel your heart opening as you raise your vibration? Is your imagination now running wild? We ask because this brings us to the third law of divine mastery and your next invitation: Use the power of your imagination—it is the force that shapes your life and defines your experience.

Everything manifested on the physical plane reflects someone's imagination. What creations have your imagination manifested so far? If you want to know how well you are using your imagination, review the creations in your present life. Admire everything you have created, good or bad, for all reflect the power of your imagination. Even painful experiences are beautiful creations. If you are not satisfied with an experience in your life, imagine it better. You improve your experiences by improving your imagination. Begin now. Breathe, smile, and open your heart. Imagination works best with an open heart. Pull your shoulders back, straighten your spine, and breathe your spirit into your body. Your life is limited only by your imagination. It is a muscle that needs to be developed. Imagination works as a container that holds your ideas, beliefs, and perceptions. If you fill this container with ideas, beliefs, and perceptions that reflect what you desire, they are attracted to your life. The same is true if filling the container with fear, sorrow, resentment, and disappointment. This, too, will be attracted to you. This is the divine law of creation.

Breathe. Connect to your light body now. Activate your imagination. It is a superpower. Begin by paying attention to what you are imagining now. Are you imagining beautiful relationships? Are you imagining a healthy body? Are you imagining a life of abundance, peace, and relaxation? One where your need for comfort and peace is met easily? Can you possibly imagine this? Those who can imagine will eventually attract this. This is the divine law.

As a light being, acknowledge the power of your imagination. Notice what you habitually imagine. Be aware of what you feed your imagination as well. Your imagination is an energetic vessel that holds images, visions, and outcomes. Are your visions beautiful, or are they nightmares projected toward you by the lowest, negative, most destructive sources, or worse? The ego has a habit of imagining the worst and holds you hostage to fear. The light body liberates and delivers you to the most glorious outcomes.

It requires effort and practice to direct your imagination how you want it to flow. Your ego will resist at first. You can overcome this resistance by consistently filling your imagination with beautiful images. Imagine that which lifts you up, makes you laugh, fills you with awe and wonder. If you don't know where to begin, look to nature. Contemplate a beautiful garden. Gaze at the night sky. Ponder the ocean tides. Breathe, and listen to the birds.

If your imagination is rusty, laden with heavy negative burdens and fears, shake them off. Release those imaginings with movement. Take a walk, a shower, dance. Do not hold on to such imaginings as if treasures to keep close to your heart.

Your Imagination Drives Your Experience into Being

These relics don't serve; they weaken you. Laugh them away and leave them behind. Your imagination will lead you toward the experiences you want. Be open to wonder, and let the adventure begin. Start each morning with wonder. Ask yourself, "I wonder what I will create today. I wonder who I'll attract. I wonder how beautiful life can become. I wonder how my spirit guides, helpers, and divine sources will assist me." Hold glorious thoughts and images in your imagination. Imagine leaving darkness behind.

Can you imagine yourself having the experiences now that you yearn to attract? This is how the divine law works. The law is to imagine first, and the experience follows. Imagine abundance first to experience later. Imagine love to experience love. Imagine health to experience health. If your imagination fails, observe the beauty and abundance found in nature, the beautiful trees outside your door, and the abundance of stars in the sky. Nature resets the imagination back to flow. Abundance is everywhere. There is no lack in the universe. There is no lack of opportunity. There is no lack of supply. There is no lack of money. There is only a lack of imagination. Reverse this and breathe in every beautiful possibility you can imagine.

Your imagination is one of your greatest powers. Indeed, it is a superpower. Use your divine power to have fun, enjoyment, and pleasure. Strengthen your imagination with play. Imagine, for example, receiving a gift. It will arrive in the next 24 hours if you imagine it well. You have this power. Use it. Take possession of this miraculous force. Wake it up and use it. Imagine from the center of your heart, not your egoic head. The intellect imagines dark shadows and casts fear. The heart infuses your imaginings with light. This is the divine law. I am Joachim, and we are the Emissaries of the Third Ray, completing our transmission for this lesson.

♦ ♦ ♦

Well, that was certainly a reminder (for me anyway) to consider how I'm using my imagination. I am excited for this lesson because I know what the Emissaries say is true. I have had the blessing and the support of great teachers who demonstrated this law. My mother was the poster child for the power of imagination; she imagined only success. And created it. She was not specially gifted with imagination either. She was practical. To her, imagination was a supply source to tap freely for all we needed. She told me from my earliest memories that all humans possess this unlimited power. She just exercised hers regularly and with great enthusiasm.

During the darkest night of my soul (over a decade ago already), my life fell apart. My brother suddenly died, and six weeks later, my father died too. Then my marriage of 33 years ended, and my finances collapsed. I had no idea how I would go on. Yet, in the middle of that implosion, my daughter, Sabrina, suggested we move to Paris. I couldn't imagine how I'd ever heal from all that loss, and yet I could imagine Paris. I didn't know how to make the move and had no rational explanation for even considering it. It made no logical sense. I couldn't even begin to explain something as crazy as this to myself, let alone others, but I *could* imagine Paris. Ninety days later, we arrived at the foot of the Sacré Cœur and moved into a charming little apartment. In that short time, I went from being a broken, shattered mess to being a resident in Paris, starting a brand-new life. I can't even remember how I got there, but I know that my imagination made it possible. It was much more enticing for me to imagine a new experience than to dwell on my losses, so that's where my attention went. I was tired of imagining the worst. I was more captivated by imagining where I would live in Paris, discovering this new city and a new me. And I found both. I am still here. Imagine that.

Your Imagination Drives Your Experience into Being

I have observed the power of imagination with students over the years as well. I remember one student, Mary Ann, a quiet stay-at-home mom of three teenagers who wanted to go back to work. She didn't go to college, so at first, she was afraid she wouldn't get hired. Her fears taunted her: "Who would want you? You don't have any skills. Younger people will take the jobs you want." But Mary Ann refused to listen. "I couldn't imagine being stuck," she said. "I only could imagine a change." She began looking on LinkedIn straight away, and the next thing she knew, she landed a commission-only sales job selling advertising on the radio.

It didn't matter that it was a commission-only job. The company motivated its salespeople with incentives, and the current sales incentive was a brand-new red convertible, a prize for the top salesperson at the end of the quarter. The possibility of owning that car captured Mary Ann's imagination. She easily imagined going from being a bored housewife in the suburbs to a rock-star saleslady tooling around town in her fancy red car. So much so that it made her laugh out loud.

Mary Ann threw herself into the job. And to everyone's surprise (except hers), she became the top salesperson month after month, even as a beginner. When the contest ended, Mary Ann was the winner. Her imagination was so engaged that everyone around her caught the buzz and wanted her to win. Her enthusiasm recruited support. When we spoke, Mary Ann shared, "Never once did I consider losing. I imagined the car was mine, and that was it. That's how it happened."

I have a two-year-old granddaughter. She is hilarious and wildly imaginative. She is such a gift to me because we have tremendous fun together. "Let's imagine we're lions. Let's imagine we're at a campfire. Let's imagine I am a superhero, and you are a cat stuck in a tree." All of that in the first 10 minutes of seeing each other. And we do imagine these scenarios and more.

When we went to the park the other day, she quickly disappeared into a grove of trees. When I caught up with her, she turned and said, "Welcome to my house." What imagination! Hers was waking up mine, and with it came forgotten joy. That's a secondary gift of imagination.

The Emissaries say we fill our imaginations. They work as a container that holds the images we put inside. What are you putting into your imagination? What am I putting into mine? We cannot create what we cannot imagine. And yet, we constantly create what we do imagine. That's the divine law.

LESSON 4

COMMITMENT IS INTENTION IN ACTION

Welcome, dear one. We delight in your presence today. You are not here on your planet by accident. You made a courageous choice to incarnate at this time, and we commend your courage. Courage and commitment are necessary components of soul mastery. This is the divine law. We celebrate your courageous commitment to your soul awakening. Your presence demonstrates that you are ready to assume your divine nature and usher light into this darkened dimension. Having made this courageous choice, commit to living as a light being. To assist in your commitment, affirm: I am a light being. I am an empowered, joyful creator. I commit to living my life through the expression of my spirit; I release the limiting confusion of the past. I am no longer trapped by matter. I am free, a butterfly out of a cocoon. I commit to expressing my beauty in all things.

Commitment is the next divine law to discover and master. Commitment is the unrestrained willingness to live as a divine co-creator, authentically and with love. Committing to living your light requires that you consciously step away from all lower third-dimension frequencies that seek to stop you from loving yourself or growing, evolving, expanding, and awakening the energetic light being you are. Once committed, be prepared for your ego to undermine your commitment: The ego will say, "Who do you think you are? How dare you change! You are full of nonsense." Your ego mind may even attack with: *"You're crazy. You're making this up. You're living in la-la land. You are delusional."* These attempts of the egoic mind to try to keep you trapped in the third dimension can be expected. Don't get caught off guard. Be prepared to defend your commitment to breaking through this pattern as you evolve into a higher frequency and ignore the ego's noise.

Living as a light being changes the way you behave in the world. Your outlook shifts when you are committed to living as a divine co-creator, a magical, miraculous, unlimited light being. Your expectations shift and change as well. When in disempowered frequencies, humans feel powerless; when you enter a higher frequency, this ceases. Doors open. Obstacles recede. Opportunities arise. Commit to your new identity, and you suddenly encounter cooperation and support. When you commit to your heart-centered self, so does life.

Commitment creates expectation. You naturally expect what you commit to show up. It will. Pause for a moment, dear ones, and consider: What do you expect from life? Do you expect miracles? Do you expect wonderful connections? Do you expect synchronicities? Do you expect gifts? Do you expect inspiration and support in all things? Do you expect to feel happy, satisfied, and fulfilled? Do you expect success? Do you expect an incredible life, or do you expect disappointment? We understand, dear ones, how easy it is to expect the worst. This is the norm of the ego in the third dimension. Overcome fear of disappointment, open your heart, and ask the universe to deliver gifts and miracles as if delivering flowers. If you fully expect these gifts, they will arrive. This is the law of the fifth dimension.

Be bold and expect support today, and you will have it. Consider the areas in which you need and would welcome support, where the old self struggles or faces disappointment. Engage the fourth law of creative mastery. Expect ease, flow, delight, and

Commitment Is Intention in Action

pleasure in the future. Expect fellow light beings to arrive with support. Expect your higher self to assist as well. Invite and invoke your available angels, guides, and the endless legions of light beings to help you. Ask them to come forward. Permit them to help you in every way. Then simply expect the best. This is how to reclaim your divinity. Expect the universe to help. The universe delivers the best when you commit to having the best. The ego expects disappointment and struggle because the ego is not your true self. It creates limitations. Commitment is necessary to expect the best. You cannot attract one without the other. Commitment is the foundation of lasting power. I am Joachim, and we are the Emissaries of the Third Ray, second octave of love. We share this transmission in a spirit of love and service.

♦ ♦ ♦

I was blessed as a child because I had quite a magical mentor in a mom. Every morning before leaving for school, she would say, "Expect good things today. I expect to hear about them when you come home." This trained me from the beginning to expect the best. Since then, I have lived my entire life expecting good things. I have not been disappointed. Good things endlessly flow my way. They can flow your way as well. When you expect good things, you commit to living as a divine being, a co-creator, a light being, not trapped in the third dimension. Expecting good things acts as a magnet. What you expect is what you get.

I had a funny experience yesterday that I want to share because we sometimes expect things through fear, which, as you may already have discovered, is an instant magnet. I live in Paris, and I have a lovely concierge who lives in my building and keeps an eye on things. Her name is Madame Tottet. I genuinely love her, and she loves me, and when we see each other, boy, do we talk. When I run into her, our chats are never quick, "Hi, how are you? Got to run!" They are 30-, sometimes 40-minute-long deep discussions. Yesterday, I was running late to meet a client, so I started fretting. *"Oh my goodness,"* I worried, *"don't let me run into Madame Tottet. I don't have time to talk to her today. Please don't let me run into her,"* I prayed, although I knew that would be tricky because it was her job to be at the front door. I was trying to wear my invisibility cloak but was so focused on running into her that the minute I entered the entrance of the building, guess who walked out? Madame Tottet. Of course she did. If only I had paused for two more seconds, she would've walked on and not seen me. But no such luck. Now for the fun part. Seeing each other, we were both surprised.

She quickly said before I could, "I'm so sorry, Sonia. I don't have any time to chat today. I've got an appointment. I've got to run." I laughed because I was trying to avoid her, fearing that she would be there; I now wondered if she was trying to avoid me as well. No wonder we ran directly into one another. Our mutual fear drew us nose to nose. It's the law.

This reminds me of another super funny moment in the past that demonstrates the same law in action. I had a student, Jill, who was so devoted to being empowered that she studied with me religiously. One day, she called and asked me to lunch, to which I agreed. This was when I lived in Chicago. While I was driving to our neighborhood restaurant, one of Chicago's famous Midwest summer thunderstorms burst upon us in a deluge. Jill shouted as we neared our restaurant, "Don't worry, Sonia! I've got this. I expect to find a nearby parking space." Sure enough, the moment she said that, someone pulled their car out within 15 feet of the front door. Then I said, "I expect a closer spot." Two seconds later, someone else ran from the restaurant and jumped into their car parked directly in front of the restaurant. We both laughed. Bam, bam. Two expectations. Two creations, one after the other. We didn't get that wet that day. That's applying law number four.

Creating with expectation is playful and fun. Expect a gift. Expect a parking space. Expect success in your presentation. Expect a wonderful evening. Expect good things. This will change your life. This will help you live as a light being. This will keep you in the fifth dimension, where you can quickly and most enjoyably create a new Earth.

Expecting something wonderful reflects aligned intention, emotion, and imagination. If you are negative, you won't expect good things. If your emotions are stuck in the past, you won't expect good things. If you don't know what you want, you won't expect good things. But when you choose to expect good things, no matter what is happening around you, good things will follow. This is the divine law. Expecting good things brings them.

LESSON 5

YOUR INNER GUIDANCE IS YOUR COMPASS

Welcome, dear one. We are so honored to have your attention. It is our privilege to escort you into the light body of who you are; we are happy to guide you into the higher frequencies of unconditional love of the fifth dimension. We are happy to encourage your expanded mind, awareness, curiosity, and heart. We invite you to bathe in the unlimited and unconditional love and support of your divine source and creator. This is the intention of the new Earth.

In the third dimension, you were trained to let your ego lead your life—your fearful, limited ego; your programmed, disempowered ego. The following divine law releases this attachment, for it simply leads to a dead end and disappointment. You are guided to follow a new compass, the heart compass, your inner guidance. Letting your heart frequency—your inner guidance, your intuition—take over is the best way to live as a light being in a light body.

Your heart compass will lead you to openings, opportunities, and divine connections. It will take you to your higher realms. Following your inner compass will lead you to delightful synchronicities, landing you at the right place at the right time. Listening to your inner voice may amount to a significant shift for you. Still, it is not a dangerous shift. Tuning in to your higher self over your fearful ego is brilliant. This involves more than listening with your ears. Listening with your heart also involves listening with your entire body. You are not listening to sound. You are listening to vibration, frequency, and energy as it keeps you aligned with your spirit and highest intent. The more you listen, the more evidence you will have that life is communicating with you. Listening with your heart allows you to sense your higher self, your divine spirit helpers, your angels, and your guides as they communicate with you. Listening with the heart attunes you to the energy behind your other thoughts and emotions. Believe the frequencies you perceive. Listen for harmony, listen for flow, listen for congruency and ease, listen for disruption, incongruency, disharmony, disruption, and move away without resistance. Listen to your light body as your divine self guides you each day. Notice how you feel the communication from the heart and inner self, making it difficult to ignore. Can you feel this communication attempting to get your attention now?

Open your heart and mind, and embrace the gift of your inner guidance. You need it to navigate energy. Your inner guidance is a gift. To ignore it is folly. To embrace it is wisdom. This is the divine law.

Listening to your inner guidance over the influences of outsiders or the second-guessing of your ego is a life-changing, transformational, and empowered decision. When you follow your inner compass over the influences of fear and control, everything shifts to more ease and flow. Your only obstacle is your resistance or reluctance to trust your divine nature.

Your inner compass functions perfectly well. It has guided you to receive this transmission. Reflect on how you came to be with us at this moment in time. It was not logic; your inner compass and your intuitive guidance led you to us. Acknowledge how often your inner guidance has helped you in the past. How

Your Inner Guidance Is Your Compass

it has kept you safe and connected you to beautiful sources of love and support. This is the function of your inner compass. Ignore all ego resistance and other unconscious interferences that would cause you to question or doubt your inner wisdom. Listening to and following your inner guidance indicates you are connected to the fifth dimension and the highest source of protection. Trust your inner guidance. It is your divine spirit speaking to you. It is the voice of your light. Listen, trust, and follow. This is the divine law. We are so honored to share our transmission on this occasion. We are the Emissaries of the Third Ray, the second octave of love.

♦ ♦ ♦

I agree with the Emissaries on the wisdom of this law. Following our intuition is the only sane decision one can make in these disruptive, ungrounded, and confusing times, as far as I'm concerned. Inner guidance is direct communication from our divine spirit. Fortunately, a collective shift is unfolding at this time, and I observe more people making the empowered, heart-centered choice to listen to their inner guidance and stop fighting it. This is a miracle. How about you? Are you increasing your willingness to follow your inner guidance? Is your inner guidance getting stronger? Are you experiencing spontaneous, intuitive downloads? Are you paying more attention to your inner light and leaving others' confusion behind? These are profound shifts worth noticing. You are evolving. Trust your spirit to take care of you. It will.

I have a client, Joe, who wanted to start a restaurant a few years ago. He had no experience. He didn't go to cooking school. He hadn't even worked in restaurants past high school. Yet he wanted to open a simple, fast-food-wraps take-out spot in his neighborhood because there wasn't anything like that around, and he liked that kind of food. His intuition told him this idea would work out, but everyone he knew told him otherwise, that it was a bad idea, bad timing, and would be a bad investment. No one supported him. Instead, he heard, "Why would you open something here? This is not a good neighborhood. You might as well throw your money away." Yet no matter how persuasive his naysayers tried to be, his intuition said otherwise, earning him criticism and rolled eyes.

Ultimately, Joe followed his intuition, and despite the deterrence he received, his "wraps shack" opened for business. It was a hit. In three short months, he recouped his initial investment. In six months, he invented an extremely popular spicy wrap, and a few months after that, Joe opened two more locations. Before listening to his inner guidance, Joe was lost. He spent a lot of time worrying about his future or doing what others told him to do, none of which made him successful or happy.

All Joe wanted to do was something fun, easy, and fast. In the end, that's precisely what he did, and to his and everyone else's surprise, it worked out well for him. Interestingly enough, those who discouraged Joe then now called him "lucky." They were unwilling to give him credit for following his heart. Joe felt disappointed in his friends who didn't celebrate him, but I wasn't surprised. True friends do celebrate you; however, people who are disconnected from their inner guidance will rarely champion others for being connected to theirs; knowing and expecting this will make it easier to ignore negativity and judgment and courageously follow your heart. There's no need to be offended if you don't get support for listening to your inner guidance. It scares people to trust their guidance, let alone champion others if they do. Please don't waste time worrying about what anybody thinks of your inner guidance, because it doesn't matter. What matters is if you let your guidance lead the way. Only you can make that decision. If you decide to follow your guidance, you must make a few big decisions to protect your choice.

Your Inner Guidance Is Your Compass

Namely, give up the need for approval from others. Also, be prepared to get pushback from others and not let it deter you. Next, you'll have to forget justifying your intuitive choices to anyone because you don't have to. Make your decisions quickly and stand by them. Assume full responsibility for yourself and your choices as a sovereign light being, and trust the outcome. This simple formula works.

I have a client, Dolores, who lives in the South in the United States. She works in construction and describes herself as a woman boss working in a good old boys club environment. Her intuition told her to start a female-owned construction company 30 years ago, and she did. Her guidance insisted that construction work suited her despite the local culture with all its machismo. In no time, she started winning contract after contract, and now, years later, she's one of the most prominent builders in the state. I'm not surprised.

In the early days of her business, Dolores encountered many people, men and women alike, who challenged her judgment. "What on earth are you doing in this world?" they questioned. She answered, "I'm building. I'm creating. I'm following my guidance." Eventually, people in the industry accepted her. In time, they came to love her. Her story is more common than not. Those who follow their inner guidance against all odds tend to succeed. Those who ignore their guidance waste time and suffer. What is your inner guidance telling you? Are you following it? And if not, why not?

It's easier to follow your guidance if you express it out loud. It is nearly impossible to ignore what you openly acknowledge. The Emissaries invite us to live in a higher, more empowered, self-directed way by faithfully listening to our inner guidance. This might feel risky to your ego. Stand behind your decisions anyway. Soon, it will be evident that this is the only way to navigate the world. It's divine law.

LESSON 6

THE LOVING UNIVERSE IS YOUR PARTNER

Welcome, dear one. We are delighted to meet again on this day. Our message is clear. The loving universe is pleased with what is occurring on your beautiful planet. Much is ending, and there is enormous chaos and disruption, yet there is no need to be frightened. A higher vibration, elevated energy, is entering, and for this to occur, the old constructs of consciousness that have shaped and formed your world must crumble. It is distressing to watch but necessary. Amid this disruption, a new world is unfolding. We do not doubt that you can sense this transformation occurring. As a result, your vibration is changing, as is your experience. Many of the principles upon which you have lived your life no longer work. The principles of the third dimension, the beliefs of the ego, which have been grounded in self-loathing, self-rejection, self-judgment, fear, and contempt for self and others, not to mention a deep disconnect from your inner light and the loving universe, are collapsing. This old programming is struggling to hold on, and in the end, it will give way to the new.

Third-dimension programming has kept many of you feeling small and afraid by affirming that you are unworthy, alone, unloved, and unsupported. It has also kept many of you stuck, isolated, and easily controlled. The new frequency now entering the planet brings with it light, love, and liberation. It makes way for the spirit in you to reenter and become embodied. Do not be surprised if you feel like you are waking from a bad dream. In so many ways, you are. Be receptive to these vibrational changes occurring in and around you. Notice how you no longer resonate with harmful and distorted self-perceptions, ideologies, and imprints. Trust your natural instinct to reject these false impressions, chains, and limitations.

Allow your spirit, your divine self, to step in and take over. This brings genuine self-love, love of your true self, and the spirit in you— not love of your ego but of your divine essence, the magnificent, miraculous light being that you are. Become aware of your divine support system. Open your heart and mind to your angels, spirit guides, higher self, and the eternal connection to the holy Mother, Father, God of the universe, your creator. Recognize yourself as a divine light being. Accept this, believe this, and live it with your whole heart, even if only for glimpses and quick moments in the beginning. With effort and practice, embodying and living your light body will become easier, more natural. You are increasingly embracing your inner light, and stepping into the fifth dimension of unconditional, joyful, celebratory love. This frequency resonates with your authentic self. Are you beginning to feel the connection to the universe? Can you sense the legions of angels who celebrate and support you, who delight in your being? Can you feel the waves of healing guides, teams of support, creative helpers, and light beings from throughout the universe surround you? Can you sense their loving frequency working to restore you and this beautiful planet Earth to its original vibration of unconditional love and light?

You are loved. You are not alone. You are infinitely and unconditionally loved and supported. We only ask that you love yourself, your true self, that you live in love, that you make decisions with love, that you follow the path that resonates love in you, and that you meet life in the frequency of love. This might well be opposite of everything you have been taught and programmed to believe *within the third dimension. Leave the old behind. Be curious and open to the new. The fourth dimension is the opening of the mind. The opening to new ideas, new expectations, new beliefs, and the ability to open and allow the spirit of the fifth dimension, the unconditionally loving you, to come in with it, as well as the help, love, and support of the entire universe.*

This new way of being, this invitation to be in love, to meet life with a loving attitude, doesn't mean being co-dependent or taking responsibility for what isn't yours. Those behaviors are not love. Those are self-punishing, self-sacrificing choices. Love liberates. Love uplifts and attracts more love. This can only occur if you begin with self-love. You cannot love outwardly if you don't love inwardly. Start with the little things you love—love that you are healthy if it is so, that you are presently safe if it is so, and that you have enough food and warmth, if it is so. Go from there. Then move to the things you love in life. Your home. Your garden. Your family. Each loving choice leads to the next; following this path, you will love life fully and freely. Your intuition will lead you to what you love and to who or what loves you.

Meeting life with love is the most potent invitation you can accept. Recognize how quickly things come to you when you love. Recognize when you fall out of love and how life comes to a standstill. You are not alone. You were never alone. Only the ego is alone. The spirit in you is divinely connected and naturally loves. Believe in what you love. Don't let the outer world tell you it has no value. Commit to what you love. Don't let anybody or anything, including your inner detractor, tell you what you love has no value.

What you love is most valuable.

Living in love is the way; it is the secret you're looking for. Living with love takes attention and practice but comes naturally to the spirit in you. Begin by loving yourself, recognizing what you love about your spirit, doing what you love to do, and being where you love to be. It starts with one question: What do you love? Listen to the answer and the vibration. Notice how love creates expansion within you. With love as your guide, everything opens up and gifts flow. Living in love elevates the entire experience of your life quickly. Love everything. Even those things that you don't enjoy. Love heals and transforms all. With love, we conclude this message. We are the Emissaries of the Third Ray, second octave of love.

♦ ♦ ♦

Letting love be the guiding value of your life is a game changer. I know it's easy when everything's going your way, but it can be more challenging when life is not going your way. I went through a difficult time years ago, when I didn't love much of anything happening. I experienced the deaths of my brother and father, and went through a divorce I didn't want. I lost my home, my neighborhood, and the life I had built. But if I were to be honest about it, everything that I lost and everything that crumbled, I didn't love. I didn't love it at all. I didn't even like most of it. It was not that I didn't love my brother and father. It was that everything was all wrong, and my spirit was asking me to grow and change.

I appreciated that my brother and father had concluded their earthly journey, and I accepted that, but what caused me the biggest frustration were the things I held on to but didn't love. Once I decided to let go of what I had built because I was not loving it, my life changed overnight. I found myself walking an 800-kilometer trail, the Camino to Santiago, across Spain, whereas up until then I had barely managed to walk to the neighborhood grocery store. That 800-kilometer journey was liberating. It redirected me in so many ways. I felt alive again. I became present. I up and moved to France, a country I had come and gone from for most of my life, and created a new me.

The Loving Universe Is Your Partner

Living in a new city, new culture, and speaking a new language had its challenges, but I loved that I was no longer trapped into being someone I didn't want to be anymore. I remembered what the Emissaries said about love, and no matter what unfolds, it is important to love the learning. I didn't enjoy much of the early experience of change. When I left my life and started over, I went through much grief and pain, but in the midst of it all, I loved that I was growing.

I have a client, Jordana, whom I just adore. When COVID hit, Jordana was in Australia and pretty much locked down and bored to death. During that time, I invited her to live a magical life, so she took that literally and taught herself magic. It was not just card tricks but really sophisticated magic, the kind she could perform.

She moved on from magic to mentalism, and after COVID-19, she used these skills in her keynote speeches on overcoming fear and living a magical life. The key to her success was that Jordana loved every minute of it. The uses of what Jordana taught herself kept growing and growing. Now she's on her way to becoming an international star. How wonderful is that? Love changed everything for Jordana. Doors of opportunity kept flying open for her. Everyone loves a lover. Her loving vibrations were infectious; others wanted to be around her. This reminds me of another love story. My sister, Soraya, went through a terrible divorce, and afterward, as a single parent of a five-year-old, struggled to keep up with work and be a good mom. One summer, she enrolled her daughter in a summer trapeze camp. She dropped her daughter off every morning and picked her up in the evening after work. One evening, Soraya was invited by the people running the camp to try the trapeze herself. The workers refused to take no for an answer, and the next thing you know, Soraya was up on the platform, high in the sky, and after receiving a lot of encouragement, took the leap.

She loved that experience so much; she couldn't believe it. She said, "I leaped into a new me." It was so life-altering for her that she signed up for their evening trapeze course that night. Guess what happened? She married the catcher who worked at the camp. Then, she joined the circus. Can you imagine how this changed her life? Love is crazy like that. Loving the trapeze experience brought her a new partner. He literally caught her in midair. You can expect to experience such miraculous shifts yourself when you do things for love and with love. And not begrudgingly, acting like you're being loving but aren't really. Only genuine love, expressed with gusto, gets these results.

After all, we're in creation school, and our number one purpose is to learn to create with love. When you choose to love everything in life, your spirit takes over, and you overcome any obstacles holding you back.

Start loving more freely and fully today. If you're not in a loving mood, then love that you are not in a loving mood. If you're having a dark night, love everything about it. If you do, it brightens. You don't have to be passionately wild about something. You can love in a low-key, nonpersonal way. If you can't conjure up joyful love, invoke nonpersonal love, and use it to learn all you can from the experiences you are in.

The more love you express in your life, the more you work with love, the more the universe will love you, show up for you, and bring you miraculous gifts—open doors, opportunities, friendships, partners, and more. If not immediately, soon enough. Loving as a life value is like finding a free ticket to board the lucky train. Accept the invitation to love. Feel the shift. It's an inside job. Love yourself first, and most, and the rest follows. It's the divine law.

LESSON 7

SURRENDER TO LOVE

Welcome, dear one. We are so happy to connect with you once again. Perhaps you are noticing that the vibration of the Earth you are used to experiencing is no longer present. Something you may not be able to name consciously has shifted, and things do not feel the same. You are accurate in recognizing this shift. The frequency of the Earth is changing. The old frequency was dark and collapsing. Its time to end has come. A tremendous infusion of light and love is now pouring into your planet. This higher frequency awakens the light body within all beings and rebalances the Earth itself. This elevated light-infused frequency is unfamiliar to many, so they may feel uncomfortable. This discomfort is your body and mind registering a difference. This may feel unsettling, even dangerous or threatening to the ego, because it is unfamiliar. Becoming accustomed to this higher frequency requires conscious attention to how you feel, what you think, the choices you make, and the creative consequences of this constellation of energies. This acute shift in awareness is not the norm for most humans who have operated at low levels of consciousness. Yet this heightened awareness is essential for both the evolution of the individual and the planet. This is the energetic transformation process.

What is happening on this planet cannot be reversed, nor would you want it to be. The awakening of the light body in humans is shifting collective values back to preserving the planet, beauty, harmony, connection, community, and cooperation among humans to live in peace within and with each other. While your ego may not understand or believe this, your spirit has elected to be here at this time to assist with this needed transformation. This is the most exciting time to evolve into a new Earth as a new human. A fifth-dimension human. A human who operates in the frequency and expression of unconditional, unlimited love: connected, loving, creative, harmonious, and peaceful.

Nothing is happening to you without your permission, however. Your free will decides and determines what experiences you allow yourself to have. You have chosen your engagements, interactions, and relationships on a soul level, for your growth. Everything is for your growth. Every invitation and opening is offered for your growth. The invitation commanding attention now is to align with your spirit, to disengage with the egoic physical self, and to live as a light being. Surrendering the ego doesn't mean giving up control of your life. It means allowing a higher energy to direct and flow through you. One that is secure, connected, expanded, creative, infinite, powerful, loving, supported, and loved.

The greatest illusion and quickest way to give up all power is to believe or say, "I have no choice." That is never true. Your will, your power to choose, is one of your greatest powers. You decide how you think, feel, act, and direct your consciousness. No one else. However, if you are disconnected from your heart and spirit, you will feel like you have no willpower. This is because your will is a function of your spirit, not your ego. So if you are disconnected from your spirit or light body, you have lost your power source, and you run on limited energy. Your spirit has infinite power, and when you allow divine will to flow through you, you have access to unlimited power.

Personal power comes by putting aside your ego and connecting with your divine self and creator. Your power is further amplified when accepting the added support of spirit helpers as you move toward your goals. This is the way of the new you, new Earth.

Accept your divine nature. Surrender your ego instead of allowing it to fight for control. Trust your divine nature and transform fear into faith. Trust all will flow, you will be guided and helped, and the outcome will be assured.

The only question is: Are you willing to allow your life to be easier? Are you willing to accept your divine nature and the unlimited love and support of the universe available to you? Are you willing to surrender ego control and trust all will be well by following your inner guidance? Are you willing to embrace a new, more powerful, less defended, fearful you? Are you willing to flow in a new way? To answer yes means surrendering ego will and embracing divine will. The ego may feel resistant, but it will surrender if you insist, and when it does, you become peaceful and confident. The ego is aware of its limitations, so it is fearful. When the higher self takes over, the ego is relieved.

Start now: Align with divine will, and trust all will unfold in your favor. Breathe. Quiet your mind. Breathe. Open your heart. Allow universal love to flow through you. Invite the ego to step aside, and let the universe support your spirit. Allow your light being to take over. Let the universe help you. Ask, "Divine Source, and all light beings, healing teams, joy guides, teachers, helpers, your holy Mother, Father, God, be at my service." We are ready and would love to be at your service. Stop fearing the goodness of life and accept the love that's trying to come through. Stop resisting the changes that you are invited to make. Stop living at a lower vibration, and instead let life flow easily. Allow the expanded light in you to shine. This light is connected, supported, loved, and loving you. It is the light of your being. Thank you for your attention to this message. We are the Emissaries of the Third Ray, the second octave of love.

That was a valuable reminder from the Emissaries. This is not the first time I've heard it either. I know that when I use my willpower instead of surrendering to a higher power, life comes to a standstill, and more problems arise. Life no longer flows. Are you aware of when this occurs in your life? For example, do you try to figure things out without success? This is a perfect example of relying on limited personal will and being disconnected from unlimited divine will, leaving you to work within limited resources. When this disconnect occurs, your brain goes around and around and around and still arrives at no solution. Working from ego will over divine will leaves you feeling frustrated, more disempowered, and trapped. I've seen and felt this powerless energy countless times. Thankfully, now I've learned.

Going back to my mom, because she was quite a great mentor, she used to say, "I don't know how this is going to work out, but it will. I invite it to work out. I'll be surprised." Things always did work out for her, and we were always delightfully surprised by how.

I recently spoke with a client, Noreen, who shared her moving story about surrendering to divine will. Her husband, Ed, died unexpectedly of a brain aneurysm, and she was left the single mother of two teenage boys and the sole breadwinner. Up until then, she was pretty much a stay-at-home mom, so she had to get full-time work—and fast—and find a means of supporting her family. Years ago, she was a therapist but stopped practicing. Now she presented small workshops, sometimes for herself and sometimes others, but it was not full-time. Noreen was in a heap of trouble for many reasons, including that her house was unaffordable. Selling it would solve her problem short term, except it presented a second problem. While her house was too expensive, all the properties she looked at were also too expensive for her budget, and she feared if she sold her house, she'd end up homeless because she couldn't replace it with something she could afford. Even if she sold hers for cash, she didn't know how she would ever find an affordable home, even with her husband's life insurance policy.

But then she remembered something I had taught her and applied it; namely, ask the universe: "Surprise me with something really wonderful, something extraordinary. Surprise me with a solution to my housing and money problem. Reassure me that this will all work out," she said out loud. After she did, she let it go, knowing this was the act of surrender she needed to allow solutions in. One day, shortly after, she was invited to co-teach a workshop in a neighboring town, something she rarely did but agreed to. On her way, she felt a strong, spontaneous, intuitive impulse to visit an open house she passed on her way to the class. Even though she was pressed for time, she followed her intuition anyway and pulled over. The house was perfect, and to her surprise, no one else was there. She put in an offer on the spot, then went on to class. To her shock, her bid was accepted, defying everything her logical brain and the market led her to believe was possible. For Noreen, this was a miracle. She demonstrated the power of surrendering personal will to divine will and then following the impulses that show up. Finding the house was a result of applying this divine law to her life.

I experienced a similar miracle recently in London, where I live part-time. My daughter, Sabrina, and her family had outgrown their little apartment but wanted to stay in their neighborhood. I helped her search for properties high and low, but at the time, there was a strange bidding war phenomenon going on, and we lost one property after another to a higher bid. One day, visiting yet another property, we shared what we were looking for with the real estate agent, who confidently and quite condescendingly said, "I've worked in this area for twenty-five years. What you're asking for simply does not exist. You're delusional." I started laughing when I heard that, rejecting what she said by replying, "I don't accept this. With all due respect, we're leaving."

Of course, she considered us rude Americans, but it didn't matter. We had to block her ego, with its negativity and limited perception. We couldn't let it get in our heads.

Two short weeks later, Sabrina called me excitedly. "I can't believe it, Mom. An apartment showed up directly across the street from you. It's exactly what we want." What was even more interesting is the owners of this apartment knew me from my work and welcomed us with open arms as the perfect people to rent the apartment to. There was no bidding war. She just got right in. It's a small, divine world where everything is possible.

This miracle unfolded because the divine law dictates that everything will work out. You don't need to know how; it'll be a surprise. It'll spare you the wear and tear of trying to figure life out unsuccessfully.

Let this divine law find your solutions instead of mentally struggling to do it yourself. There's only one requirement: surrendering ego control and being willing to trust the universe to take over. Whatever you want, whatever you yearn for, trust the universe will make it happen if you're willing to allow it. The simplest way to put this into practice is to say to the universe, "Surprise me with the solution." This doesn't mean being passive. Take the actions you need to make what you want to happen, happen. Still, always leave room for the universe to work out the details, revealing the best solution possible. It will.

A New Way of Being

Let's pause for a moment and review the first seven divine laws of creative mastery. The Emissaries present these laws as an invitation to shift our consciousness and live in the flow of our true nature as light beings. The Emissaries also point out what many sensitive people know to be true. Despite the uncertainty and discomfort of the changing vibrations of the planet, we are leveling up. We are evolving while simultaneously purging old perceptions and patterns that have trapped us in the third dimension of fear and separation. The new way of being differs from anything we've learned or been told before. It asks us to see ourselves in our true essence as divine light beings. Let's take a moment to assess where you find yourself along the learning curve with these laws.

Breathe and reflect. Begin with divine law number one: *Intention is power.* Do you accept your intention is your power and your life is your creation? Do you believe your intentions direct your experiences? Are these first seven divine laws familiar, or are they entirely new? If they are new, you are in the student stage. If this is where you find yourself, keep learning. It gets more and more exciting as you do. If these laws are somewhat familiar, but you forget to apply them, or are uncertain how to, you are in the apprentice stage. Look for role models and teachers who inspire you and follow their example. If you are pretty familiar with these seven divine laws and are fully committed to applying them to your life, then you are in the journeyman stage. If in this stage, carry on and experiment. You learn best by doing. If you know with certainty that you will succeed in whatever you put your mind to, then you are mastering these seven laws, and whether you know it or not, living with such confidence will allow you to serve as a teacher for those around you.

If you're a student, continue to gather information. Read. Listen to those who are evolving. Open your mind and heart to this new way. Trust where your heart and spirit lead you. If you're an apprentice, follow your inspirations, study those who inspire you, and reflect the same behaviors. If you're a journeyman, track your success. Notice what works for you and continue. Learn as you go. And if you're a master, inspire the struggling people around you.

Breathe and reflect once again. Let's move on to the next divine law: *Feelings are your fuel.* What about your feelings? Do you recognize how they are your fuel? Are you releasing heavy emotions to make way for lighter, brighter emotions to fuel you? Are you feeling more present, seeking more of what lifts you—like music, beauty, art, and nature? If you're emotionally most often in a funk right now, it simply means you are in the student stage of the second law. Continue to learn more about how emotions fuel your life, and it will naturally move you into the apprenticeship stage. If you recognize that your emotions don't have to control you, that you can release them instead of holding on, yet you continue to struggle with your emotions a little bit, with some days feeling better than others, you have entered the apprentice stage of the second law. You're on your way. Continue to seek teachers, mentors, helpers, and healers to assist in ushering in positive, uplifting, energizing experiences.

If you feel more present, enjoying life more today, and consciously choosing what feels good while walking away from what doesn't, you've entered the journeyman stage. It's exciting to know how quickly you are progressing to mastery. Continue to seek and do what feels deeply satisfying and less of what does not. Following this simple formula, you will soon master this law.

The same goes for your imagination. Breathe and reflect. Are you drowning in negative imaginings? Not to worry. You are in the student stage of this law. Don't judge. Simply become more aware. Notice what your imagination is holding on to. Empty the imaginings that depress and deflate your spirit. The more you fill your imagination with beautiful images, feelings, and energies, the more quickly you enter the apprentice phase. In this phase, consciously seek and hold on to uplifting imaginings and people who fill your imagination and inspire you. With their beautiful influence, you advance to the journeyman stage. In this stage, select only that which inspires you while easily leaving the rest behind. The journeyman phase is incredibly empowering. The more you fill your mind and heart with imaginings of love and beauty, the more quickly you master creating this beautiful life for yourself.

As you can see from these examples, each divine law naturally carries you from one stage to the next and from one law to the next with ease and grace. This is the natural design of the universe working in a harmonious, beautiful order. We are all in various stages of learning the divine laws. No one is alone. We're all in this together. We're all evolving. We're all helping one another. We all have the support of a loving universe to help us.

Now let's move on to the second set of seven divine laws.

PART II

NEW BEHAVIORS

LESSON 8

BECOMING PRESENT

Dear one, can you feel the rays of light pouring in on you? Can you feel the transformational shifts occurring within you, overriding fear and bringing with them waves of positivity, optimism, and joy? They come in waves, these new frequencies, and you must adjust. The old identities that have been so entrenched and ingrained in you are resistant; focus and make your heart available to your guides' support to make your return to spirit easier.

Do not approach growth the old way: with fight and struggle. The new way is creative, curious, and filled with wonder. Reassure your ego: It's okay; we are all learning something new. Don't fight. Don't fear. The best way to achieve this transformational shift and eliminate the ego's resistance is to practice being present.

The ego mind is rarely present. It is preoccupied either with past experiences that have already come and gone, and the ego is trying to rewrite them, or it is projecting into the future, trying to control what is to come, based on fears from a disappointing past.

There is another state of mind in which to live. There is another state of consciousness in which to exist. That state of mind is called being present. Imagine that you, as the egoic mind, are traveling horizontally in life, moving from frame to frame of experience like clips of a film, giving the illusion that you are going somewhere; now imagine that instead of living in this linear, third-dimension fashion, that you come back to your breath, back to your spirit, and that you are now traveling through life vertically rather than horizontally, lifting out of the dense frequency of the third dimension, rising through the mind, first entering the fourth dimension, and discovering your nonphysical self. Imagine that you continue to rise vertically and eventually enter the fifth dimension, an even more light-filled, loving frequency where you experience yourself as spirit surrounded by unconditional love and connected to everything, including your beautiful Divine Creator. Can you possibly imagine the joy this would bring?

Entering the fifth dimension is no more difficult than this exercise. Your spirit rightfully resonates with the fifth dimension, and you can immediately enter by simply being present. Being present is one of the more demanding challenges of consciousness, and it is a state that comes and goes. Yet the more you practice being present by noticing what is beautiful right before you, you begin to train your egoic mind to relax and let your spirit take over. You have just slipped into the fifth dimension. Being present is where all true power lies. Being present is being free of fear, allowing the energy of your divine self to flow through you right now; you being present allows you to automatically recognize the divine light shared in all things and beings. Fully present awareness creates a transformational shift in your thinking. Recognizing the spirit in all things ends isolation and fear of others. You embrace your true nature as a divine light being. This reconnection relieves the ego of fear and gives you access to unlimited power.

Take a moment and look up now. What is the most beautiful thing right before your eyes? The egoic mind scans for the worst, expecting it to come around. This is how the human survival brain functions. When in your light body, however, you notice instead what is beautiful before you. Of course, the egoic mind will argue, "What do you mean, focus on what is beautiful? I'm having a horrific experience. The Earth is crashing; people are suffering and dying. Nothing's beautiful." This is not so. This is a selective outlook; yes, much is crumbling that needs to crumble. There is suffering, and humans are learning from this. This cannot possibly be understood in the third dimension, yet all souls have agreed to take part in all that unfolds in their lives, for the sake of their learning and for what it can teach others.

Being present means looking beyond the surface of life. It means looking for the spirit in life, starting by the spirit in you, being one who beholds the goodness of life. As you retrain your consciousness to recognize the spirit, the beauty in all things right now, you open the way for the spirit to create more of the beauty you behold. This doesn't ask you to deny the crumbling of the old, but to see it isn't the only thing happening. Notice the new emerging life unfolding at the same time.

Practice being present. Pause. When your mind is troubled, look up and notice the most beautiful thing to behold right now. Appreciate it. Let it in. Receive it into your heart. Receive it into your body. It, too, is real. It is trying to support you. Receive, open, and allow. Feel your guides, feel your creator. Feel their presence. Feel how life is trying to nurture you. The new version of you, the new flowering of you, is coming in; be present to this. Being present takes practice. But this simple practice is quite enough. We are the Emissaries of the Third Ray, the second octave of love.

Learning to be present has been one of the most demanding yet rewarding practices I learned with my spiritual teachers' help. One of my favorite sayings from one of my teachers is that everything we see is true but incomplete. When I began my training with my master teacher, Charlie Goodman, whom I've written about in many of my books, he showed me images of humans having various experiences. Some were horrible images of suffering, fires, illnesses, and accidents. I was appalled when seeing these. How awful. I would cry and cringe. Then he would say, "Sonia, the human journey can be a painful experience, but it is important to look past the surface to the eternal light having that experience. Every one of us has our own journey, sometimes fraught with tremendous challenges, and yet every experience brings infinite value. The ego will never understand, but we must recognize that these experiences serve the spirit's growth, the awakening of the light body, and the growth of consciousness." From this, I learned how important it is to observe things from more than a subjective perspective. It was and still is a difficult lesson for me. One that has been especially challenging in the last few years. It seems we humans are experiencing one catastrophic upheaval after another. So many things are so extremely challenging. Unprecedented events have upended our sense of safety and security, beginning with the pandemic, moving on to climate changes, political upheaval, and unimaginable wars, coupled with tremendous losses of life and damage to the planet; these third-dimension catastrophes have wreaked havoc on so many lives in every way, not to mention have destabilized the ego in all of us.

But if we look past all of this and into the spirit of things, we can sense and even see new life emerging. New things are being born—new ways. For example, never before have I met so many open hearts and encountered so many people interested in and available to their intuition. Never have I witnessed or encountered so many people talking about self-love, healing the past, forgiving others, addressing PTSD, and nurturing themselves. And seeking ways to connect and be kinder with and to fellow human beings. This is all mirroring the new human, new Earth the Emissaries are talking about.

This law asks us to become present to all that is happening, including all that is good. We are being encouraged not to be mesmerized and appalled by what is falling apart but to be fully present to the emerging higher consciousness and beauty of the moment. The more present we are, the more beauty we call forward. Soon, instead of being mesmerized by the old crumbling, the more we will be in awe of the birth of the new Earth. Look up right now and search for the most beautiful thing before you. Do this 10 times a day until it becomes second nature. Soon it will be what you look for and see most of the time. Soon beauty will be the thing you never overlook.

Being present doesn't come easily, but with practice, it does become second nature. If asked, "What's the most difficult thing in your life right now?" without missing a beat, most people will have at least 10 things to share. "This went wrong, and that went wrong, and this went wrong too." Ask the same people what is good and beautiful in their lives, and their responses may not come as readily.

I have a client, Isabel, whose biggest sorrow is that while she's become quite a renowned speaker in her field as a therapist, her father refuses to acknowledge anything she does, nor does he consider what she's accomplished to have any value. Her purpose in life, according to him, is to get married before it's too late, stay home, and have a family. Anything other than that, in his mind, is a failure. Isabel and I talked about her sorrow for months, noting her need for his approval (which was not coming) kept her feeling small, and far from truly celebrating who she is and the beauty she brings to the world. No matter her success, she felt like an imposter and a failure. It boiled down to, "Because you're not recognized by your father in the past, you invalidate yourself now." Yes, she regrettably acknowledged, her ego was defeated.

A couple of months ago I spontaneously asked her, "What's the most wonderful thing that has happened recently?" At first, she hemmed and hawed, trying to think of something. Then, as if a light popped on, she brightened a little and said, "As a matter of fact, my parents recently had a huge argument, and my mom, who does recognize my talent as a therapist, asked for my input. Shockingly, they both listened to what I had to say. Later, my father wrote and thanked me, saying, "I had no idea you were so brilliant. You really helped us." Isabel continued, in a rather bland voice, "When I read that, I was surprised." And that's all she said. She barely registered the miraculous shift that just unfolded. The father who never acknowledged her finally did. But it barely made a dent in her perception or story. When sharing this, she didn't say a great thing had happened. It took her a few minutes to recall this at all. When I pointed out that it was quite the miracle, her response was, "Oh, I guess you could say that." But I wasn't going for it. I wouldn't let her ego rob her of this transformational moment as if it were no big deal, one that would change her entire inner story and give her the acknowledgment she'd craved for years and years. "Wait a minute, wait a minute," I pushed back. "You had a miracle, and you're acting like you can barely remember it, let alone acknowledge that it made any difference in your life. What's up with that?"

Looking at it from my point of view, she laughed and said, "You're right. That is actually pretty crazy, isn't it?" This is an example of how the ego keeps distracting you and keeps you addicted to misery. This law is about intercepting the ego's sabotage, practicing being present and noticing what good thing is happening right now. And if it's nothing more than "I'm breathing," it's better than not breathing. It's better than being dead. Some of you might debate this, but you're still here. That's what this lesson is about. Notice what you're noticing. Are you preoccupied only with a distant or miserable past, a miserably imagined future? Or can you notice what is beautiful right now? The more you notice, the more you will notice the beautiful, offering evidence of the new world unfolding before our eyes. It's pretty exciting and pretty wonderful. It's the law.

LESSON 9

BE QUIET AND LISTEN

Welcome, dear one. We are so excited to be present to your evolution, to the awakening and indeed witnessing of your growth, empowerment, and return to your divine nature. It is happening more quickly than you know; you are not alone in this emergence. The entire universe celebrates your awakening. As you return to spirit, you become part of the healing of this planet. You become part of the beauty. You become one of the bringers of the new Earth. We honor and encourage you because this has been a challenging experience. Once again, we invite you not to approach these times from the perspective and practices of the third dimension, fighting and struggle.

We encourage you to adopt new behaviors of quiet and surrender and allow your divine spirit to step in to bring wisdom and calm. This requires retreat, stepping from the noise of the outer world, to going inward, being quiet, and listening internally to the heart, the spirit, and the creator. This, for many, is known as the practice of meditation.

To meditate, simply be quiet for a few minutes each day. Welcome a retreat from the outer world. Make it a priority. Be wary of the intrusions of the outer world; prioritize your inner peace and quiet. Create an atmosphere, and adopt an attitude that moves away from outer intrusions and into inner communication. This does not require that you become hermetic or monk-like. Simply understand you need peace as much as you need oxygen and food.

Inner quiet feeds and fuels the spirit in you. It reconnects you to your source and nourishes your essence and your body.

Be mindful of what you listen to, as it takes energy and allows vibration in. You absorb the energy of what you listen to like a sponge: dissonant noise, conversation, attitude, opinion. All are disturbing to the spirit. Silence is best. When you silence the outer world and turn inward, you attune to the power of your heartbeat. When quiet, your divine healers can restore your body and bring it back into coherence, back into harmony and congruency with the love and light of the universe. Find quiet through listening inward. Instead of being distracted by the outer world, let quiet nourish you and preserve your peace. Quiet is as essential to your well-being as food, rest, and even breathing are to your physical body.

There is a whole universe waiting to speak with you, to nourish you, to heal you, to inspire you, to delight you, to inform you, to protect you when you go inward. Meditation is a beautiful practice, but it may not come easily to you. If you cannot sit quietly and still your mind, go inward with a breath and ask your spirit, "How do I achieve peace? How can I find a connection with my inner light?" Then listen to your heart. Your spirit may suggest that you go for a walk, work in a garden, listen to beautiful music. You may be guided to journal, as peace may come through your writing. There is no correct way to find peace. There is no proper meditation. Ask your spirit to show you your way to peace. Ask your spirit to guide you, strengthen you, and connect you to Source. The outer world is noisy and confusing. You cannot stop this noise, but you certainly have the power to stop paying attention to it.

Choosing more quiet will heal you, body, mind, and spirit. Create time to go inward. Do this frequently throughout each day. Turn away from outer distractions. Turn inward. When you feel lost, exhausted, anxious, and afraid, go inward. Be quiet. You will find the light and the way. You will receive what you need. You will be restored. This is the law. We are the Emissaries of the Third Ray, the second octave of love.

❖ ❖ ❖

Be Quiet and Listen

Being quiet and listening inward have been the foundation of my emotional and mental and physical health. I learned this from my teachers when I was one year old. I had beautiful teachers who showed me that turning my attention away from the outer world was the most powerful self-care and intuitive strengthening choice I could make.

My teacher, Charlie, whom I've written about in many of my books, was a trained theosophist, mystic, and intuitive master teacher. He taught me to meditate when I was 12 years old. I just giggled and laughed through this first lesson, but he was undisturbed. He kept breathing, eyes closed, and chanting "om" in his loud, booming voice, which made me nervous. Eventually, my ego settled down, and I started breathing with him, then matching his chant. Suddenly, I relaxed and felt the presence of my guides. I felt my higher self. I felt my connection to Source. I experienced what he was talking about. I didn't have to imagine it. I *experienced* it.

I was lucky to learn to be quiet and go inward when I was so young. I've seen how others suffer for not knowing how to be internally quiet. One of my clients, Daniel, was in an accident at work last year. He worked at a construction site, and one day, a large piece of equipment crashed to the ground right next to him. It was so loud he lost his hearing for three or four months. It gradually returned, but at first, he panicked, fearing it was lost forever. I can understand why. Losing any physical sense is traumatic. But once he stopped struggling and accepted his fate, he asked me how he could better deal with what was happening. I shared something that my teacher once shared with me: "No matter what is happening in your life, the most powerful thing you can do is embrace it as an opportunity to learn, and love learning from it." I then asked him what he might learn from this accident. He said, "I want to learn to be quiet. I guess I now have my chance."

He took his hearing loss as an invitation. Not being able to hear sound wasn't the same as being quiet. He knew that was an inside job. Daniel started meditating for a few minutes at a time. Eventually, he asked me how to listen to his heart, and I offered a few tools for him to try, mostly centered on breathing. As he was convalescing, he said, "I'm actually starting to hear an inner voice, just as you promised I would. In fact," he continued, "it isn't a voice. It is more of a feeling energy vibey thing." He couldn't quite explain. It didn't matter. "You don't have to explain this to anyone, Daniel. It's your inner voice," I reminded him. Later, he shared more. "When I got quiet, I realized I was angry, judgmental, negative, and so aggressive. I'm not surprised that that accident happened to me. My energy was similar to the crash I experienced. I've decided to tone down the drama and get calm. I'm practicing being quiet. I've stopped talking so much, and I'm listening far more. I don't even care if my hearing returns. I've got my peace back."

Fortunately, Daniel's hearing returned, yet he received a double blessing from this accident. He discovered that inner dialogue can be far noisier than the outer world, and if not quieted, we won't be able to hear our inner guidance.

Before we finish this lesson, choose to listen to your inner guidance. Pick a time of day and set aside an amount of time to be quiet and then keep it. You can be silent for five minutes and listen. That can be extended to 10. It's not so much the quantity of time but the quality of time that matters. Set the intention to make this moment of quiet your new way of being. Stop talking. Start listening to your heart. It's a divine law.

LESSON 10

ALL IS IN
DIVINE ORDER

Dear one, are you enjoying this beautiful shift of consciousness? Are you excited, delighted, and in awe of this human creation? Can you feel our presence? Can you feel your power? Are you experiencing the healing flow of love from you and to you? Have you noticed the energy of fear and restriction is holding less and less of your attention? These are indeed exciting times. You are lifting out of the third dimension. You are indeed awakening these higher dimensions of awareness in you. You are becoming a new human in the new Earth. A new soul, an awakened spirit embodied.

Notice the shifts in your feelings. Notice the optimism. Notice the focus. Notice how you are no longer so quickly unconscious and in automatic reaction to the world. Are you sensing a stronger connection to your inner guidance? Even though your ego mind may still be cautious and fearful, don't let this interfere with your confident flow. Are you noticing your humor returning? We invite you to recognize these shifts unfolding in the present moment. Most of all, we encourage you to notice the hidden connection in all things. In doing this, feelings of isolation and disconnection begin to subside. Have you noticed that as soon as you think of something, it begins to occur? Have you noticed when someone enters your mind, a short time later, they will either connect with you through the phone or in a chance encounter? Have you noticed signs on billboards, in books, and even on radio broadcasts that communicate precisely what you need or reveal what you are looking for at the perfect time? Welcome to the fourth and fifth dimensions, the new Earth, where you begin to experience a connection to all things in a delightful and even humorous way.

We who exist in the subtle realms of the fourth and fifth dimensions are communicating with you at all times. We are angels, joy guides, nature spirits, teacher guides, and higher selves. Among us are beloved departed family members, light beings, healers, and the holy Mother, Father God. We are so delighted that you are noticing our presence, as we seek to reassure you that all is well and in divine order. Let our presence and support become part of your daily reality. The more you ask for and accept our help, the more readily you will create all that you need to be secure and at ease. We offer guidance if asked, assistance as well; we do not interfere with your free will. We will point your attention in the direction of opportunity and away from harm if you request our assistance. This is our purpose. This is the way of the fourth and fifth dimensions. This is the way of unconditional love. Your new way.

Notice and embrace the divine support coming your way. Do not allow your ego to doubt or dismiss our loving assistance. We will not interfere with your free will. Ever. Our communication is gentle, leaving room for you to either embrace or reject it. Again, our primary purpose is to assure you all is in divine order. Live as a divine co-creator, a child of the universe, and the path to everything you need at any time will be made clear. You are limited only by your imagination.

Recognize the sublime organization and order of the universe. Notice how chaos gives way to order, a beautiful symphony and choreography of events unfolding in your favor. Disappointment serves only to redirect you to a better path and higher opportunity. Everything is serving to elevate and support a more joyful

All Is in Divine Order

experience. Release your fear, resistance, and control, and recognize how the universe is flowing your way, bringing gifts and opportunities. Notice how infinitely and lovingly the universe works on your behalf. We are the Emissaries of the Third Ray, second octave of love and this is divine law.

When you stop looking for what's wrong with life and start recognizing what is working in your favor, you are leaving the third dimension and starting to live as a divine light being.

I had an experience not too long ago with a client, Louise, who had been through many dramas and traumas in her life, all centered around an ambitious but dark, power-hungry father. Louise lived on Maui in a plantation home she had inherited from her father after much fighting with siblings and stepsiblings in court. Louise recently lost that home in the explosive Maui fires, an unexpected and tragic event for thousands. Interestingly enough, Louise confessed that owning that home was not a blessing, citing the endless resentments from others regarding how the house came to be and the abuse that it was built on, including fraud and deceit of the local people who had originally owned the land. Louise's home was not the beautiful vacation oasis it appeared to be to the outside world. It had a dark, unhappy history that haunted the place. Louise didn't want it, yet her inheritance stipulated that she couldn't sell it. Long before the fire came, Louise had prayed to the universe to help her get out of it.

Then, the house burned to the ground. Quite remarkably, her prayers were answered. She was not the only one who felt this was a blessing. Her siblings did too. What was a loss for so many was their liberation. "We are sifting through the aftermath. It is still painful. All our family memories were lost. There is much grief, but for the first time, we are now not fighting. It's a miracle." Louise offers us a reminder that all human experience is temporary, and loss is an inevitable part of it.

When we notice that growth follows loss, that there's always a gift to be found, as painful as it is, we begin to understand how life and the universe work. We are all here to learn to manifest and create but also to let go just as readily.

We come from the spirit, and we return to the spirit, and nothing in the physical plane goes with us. It can be acutely distressing to experience this simple truth when we are in the midst of loss. With loss, there are painful emotions to process. I experienced this when I went through the death of my father and brother; the end of my marriage; and the loss of my home, community, and financial security all within six months. At the time, I thought I'd never get past the pain, but in the end, it gave me the freedom to live a more authentic life (although it took a while to come to that realization). Loss is indeed an inevitable part of the human experience, and yet opportunity follows all loss.

I recall another client, Catherine, whom I worked with a while back. She shared: "I was planning on going into business with a friend, and we were well into the planning stage. On one of our brainstorming calls, he casually mentioned something that indicated to me he was having second thoughts, a huge red flag for me. All he said was, 'Gee, I hope I can do this.' It was a casual comment, and we kept going on. But I noticed in it a lack of commitment and intention. It was so strong that I couldn't ignore it. His words didn't match his energy, so we had to stop right there. The next time we spoke, I confronted him. 'I have to ask: Do you intend to go through with this?' Surprised, he immediately responded with, 'Well, yes, if this happens and this happens,' and many excuses and qualifiers. I said, 'That answers my question; we're not going to do this.' I called it off." Catherine said, "I spared myself from making a commitment with the wrong partner. What I felt was not disappointment and upset, but relief. I also realized I didn't want a partner myself. I had talked him into it because I was afraid of going into business alone. He helped me find the confidence to admit this. His hesitation was a gift. I am now in business for myself and enjoying it completely." The point of this story is to pay attention to all clues, however subtle, rather than ignore them. They reveal the truth. Be honest when you notice such clues as well. Catherine could have gotten upset and said, "You're wasting my time." But that would've been her ego not being honest either. When she noticed her friend's hesitation, she noticed her own as well. From this, she made the best decision for both of them.

When you start noticing how life is talking to you, when you see a bus go by with a billboard that says, "Don't stop believing," for example, and you know that message is meant for you, you have entered the fifth dimension. When you are invited to do something you'd normally refuse, and yet your inner voice says, "Go," and you do, leading to a great opportunity, you are starting to flow with the universe. You are leveling up to the higher dimensions of ease and flow. Life will undeniably get better.

That happened to one of my clients, Bea, who was recently invited to dinner. She didn't want to go for a lot of reasons. "I'm tired after work. I didn't know those people. I wanted to binge watch TV." Yet her inner voice pushed back and said "Go," so she did. That night she met the man she married. Bea was well into her late forties and had long written off getting married. She wasn't even looking for a partner. Evidently, the universe had other plans for her. This demonstrates that wonderful things begin to occur when you notice and follow the signs. Noticing and recognizing signs always works in your favor. You enter the flow. To integrate this law into your life, notice one thing that worked in your favor today. Acknowledge something, however subtle. Pay attention instead of ignoring life communicating with you, and soon, it will magically improve in every way. This is the law.

LESSON 11

A GIFT IN EVERYTHING

Dear one, these are indeed exciting and transformative moments in your life. We clearly observe your evolution as you enter the full embodiment of your divine spirit. Indeed, it is a dramatic and joyful shift to behold. We humbly continue to suggest new behaviors leading you further into these higher dimensions. Today's suggestion is to see that everything that unfolds in your life is a gift. Not to the ego, perhaps, for the ego does not experience much of anything as a gift. Everything is a gift from your spirit to your spirit.

You are here in creation school to master being a spiritual, embodied co-creator. Everything you experience contributes to achieving your success. This, of course, refutes the conditioning of the ego in the third dimension. The ego experiences everything in life as a challenge, potentially a threat, a danger. As you evolve into a higher dimension of you, a higher, more evolved expression of you, the fear of loss begins to subside. Have you noticed being less bound by time and space? Are you yet losing the fear of death? Are you recognizing the human physical journey is indeed temporary, but the spirit is eternal? When you do, you realize life is no longer something to fear but to enjoy.

As you evolve into these higher frequencies and vibrations, you gain confidence. You sense what rings true for you in the very center of your being. When you meet life as if everything it brings you is a gift, including loss, disappointment, and heartbreak, and you achieve the freedom to love, if you embrace everything as a gift, there is nothing to fear. There is no loss to fear, only change of expectations to accept. When everything is a gift, you trust what comes your way is aligned with your true nature, more fulfilling, more joyful, more than what your ego had planned for you. We realized this requires a complete reorganization of your perspective, your priorities, your sense of safety, and your idea of success. The spirit in you is infinitely creative and powerful. It brings success in surprising ways. The gifts of spirit ripple beyond your personal enjoyment and contribute to the world.

The Emissaries invite you to bring to mind your most recent hurt, wound, or disappointment. The pain you hold most dear in your heart. Please now unwrap this pain and look with the fresh eyes of spirit. Search for the gift. What gift has come from this pain? What does this sorrow offer? When you see and receive the gift, the pain subsides. If the gift is not immediately obvious, know in your heart that in time, it will be. Acknowledge the gifts of pain, and embody their blessings. They belong to you and will serve you later. They're there for your growth. They will bring you peace and freedom in time. This particular lesson is challenging to many of you because you are experiencing so much loss. Much is crumbling, making it easy for the ego to suffer. "I don't see any gift in this." Be patient and compassionate. This will pass, and liberation will take its place. We are the Emissaries of the Third Ray, the second octave of love.

This isn't the first time I've been reminded of this lesson. The Emissaries have been with me for some time, and I remember at one point after having just moved to Paris, after I'd lost my home, went through a terrible divorce, and experienced financial ruin, the Emissaries reminded me that one day I would consider all these losses a gift. It angered me at the time. I was in no mood to notice the gifts. Not only that, but

I had moved to Paris with my grown daughter, Sabrina, and she suddenly fell in love with a man she met in London, so she left too, which I experienced as more loss. I hadn't envisioned myself being here all alone. I didn't see the gift in my unexpected isolation. But I did spend many days walking the city of Paris, and frankly, that was a gift because it was so beautiful. While walking, I realized that this was the first time in my life when I was alone. I was born a middle child of seven. I never even had a door on my bedroom growing up. I got married young to someone who was the oldest of nine, so his energy overwhelmed my own. I found myself living in the middle of a mosh pit of others my entire life. In fact, it wasn't until my 30s that I even referred to myself as "I." I was always a part of "we."

Being alone and not lonely was a surprise. I experienced the gift of boundaries and self-love and appreciation. My aloneness freed me from the co-dependency that came with living in a group experience. My new single status offered the gift of feeling whole and complete without being in a relationship. I realized I enjoyed my own company in this beautiful place on earth. I didn't feel isolated. I could call anybody anytime on FaceTime. In fact, I was deeply loved. Lots of those loving people wanted to visit me. The only lonely place existed in my head. My gift was reframing the past from one of terrible loss to incredible liberation. Truthfully, my ego didn't notice any of these gifts for some time. But my spirit did right away. I went back and forth from a third- to a fifth-dimension perception. I was on an emotional roller coaster ride for some time. Eventually, my emotions leveled out and peace followed. I share this because noticing life's gifts is messy, and it's okay to go through lots of difficult emotions and reactions and negativity before you see or accept them. Just know in time gifts come.

I have another client, Vicky, who went through a divorce 20 years ago. In her situation, her husband left her for her best friend. She felt so wounded that she forgot that she didn't like her husband or her best friend and was happy to be rid of them both. Sadly, Vicky remained stuck on the betrayal story and couldn't get past it. She became so angry with me when I asked her to find "the gift," that I backed away. I stopped suggesting this to her. I asked instead, "What's the gift in staying stuck? You're pretty committed to it, so what is the payoff?" "The payoff," she responded without missing a beat, "is that I don't have to take responsibility for this mess or my life. My ex-husband has to do that, and my ex-best friend still has to feel guilty while I just sit here. This feels great for now."

That was enough of a gift for Vicky, so I let it be. I never brought it up again. But I learned, people do what they want. Leave them to it.

The last time I spoke with Vicky, she said, "Sonia, I'm not angry anymore. I'm not dwelling on the past either. I went back to school, and I love it. I'm learning art, and I'm happy being me." This shows you that you don't have to identify a gift quickly. It helps if you do, but if you need time to process, to receive the gift, to take it in, take all the time you need. A gift always follows a loss, and yours is waiting for you.

Take the time, grieve your losses, and be honest. Whatever unfolds, the soul expects to get something valuable from it. The sooner you notice what gift is emerging, the more empowered and peaceful you will be.

Noticing soul gifts may be new to you. Recognize that loss always opens the door to a higher dimension and will bring tremendous power. Test this right now. Recall the most painful thing you've experienced while seeing it as the most beautiful gift you've ever received. When this is easy to do, you're embracing this divine law.

LESSON 12

LOOK PAST APPEARANCES

Dear one, your evolution is quickening, your transformation unfolding. Do not be surprised at the rapidity of change. Do not be surprised at how quickly your transformation is occurring, for the entire universe is moving in this direction for the evolution of not only the Earth but also your being in the new Earth. As you activate the fourth and, indeed, the fifth vibrational dimension, you also spontaneously begin to awaken the long-dormant perceptions of the intuitive channels. You no longer look at life. You begin to see beyond appearances into the forces of energy, into the hidden aspects of all things. This is the basis for the skill known as clairvoyance—clear view.

We invite your behaviors to shift away from looking simply at the surface of life, which does not reveal a true and whole picture, which does not reveal what is actually in play in every scenario. Looking at life can often appear to be a very horrifying, depressing, sorrowful experience because it is temporary. When you look into and see beyond the surface and into life, you begin to see the eternity of all things, the beauty of all things, and that there is no finality. You also begin to recognize that you learn and see and understand according to your level of consciousness and the commitment to being conscious. A soul that is a student may still see through the lens of victimhood: Why is this happening to me? Why are you doing this to me? Not seeing their own free will and the gift of growth, which is very different from a master who will see the same experience looking for the gift, looking for the growth. Oh, I understand this is unfolding because it is a warning; it is a lesson. It is an opportunity to grow. It is an invitation to realign to something even more accurate for my spirit's happiness, something more coherent and congruent.

Learning to see with clairvoyant eyes will begin to not only show you a depth of truth and what intentions are operating behind appearances, but it will also become a protective force, for as we know in the unconscious outer world, people say what they do not mean. People do things that do not align with their true heart. It is a confused and distorted, chaotic experience. But when you work with the inner eye, you begin to see through all of this myriad of confusing energies and see your path forward with free flow. When we say look past appearances, we do not mean simply working with your inner eye. You can see with your whole body, just like you can hear with your whole body; you can see an outcome. You can see a path forward; you can see a solution without it actually taking on a visual form. It is a comprehension and understanding of the way to proceed as a creator. So, as you work to awaken the higher self, to awaken the spirit, to master the soul, you understand that the vision you're awakening is the true and most aligned path that is congruent with your soul, that there is nothing working against you. There are energies working in their own interests, and it's for you to step aside when you sense, not just see but perceive incongruencies, perceive harmonies, perceive resonance, perceive dissonance.

Just as you've awakened in the intuition, the inner ear, now we awaken the inner vision. Part of this experience that is so exciting is that you will now begin to awaken to what you call downloads. Downloads are gifts from your higher self, giving you the vision that is most congruent with your soul, giving you the understanding of what is operating behind appearances, giving you insights to how things are unfolding, giving you opportunity to see what is not obvious to the eye but is nevertheless available to you. Are you interested and available to seeing more than meets the eye? Can you see the spirit unfolding in all things? Can you see the wisdom of the universe guiding you? Are you willing to be shown new visions?

This is a new approach, a new behavior, a new way of living, and you recognize how this is starting to spontaneously occur. Notice how, for example, in the relationship that has frustrated you so much that you have deemed the other person a narcissist, or you have deemed them a wounded, addicted person. All of a sudden, you see beyond their effect on you. Someone truly suffering and struggling gives you the understanding that you will not get from this person what you want, nor will you take it personally. You are simply in the experience of their own chaos affecting you. That is what we are inviting you to do now, to look for the truth beyond appearances—what is really occurring and why? Let your spirit be the vision that reveals to you a deeper understanding of everything, and you will suffer less. You will also notice you are attached to less because you also see in yourself that you are whole and complete. That relationships are benefits to co-create, but not fundamental needs for survival as your ego itself. What have you believed that, as you begin to see the truth in the outer world and in others, you also see in you? I am whole and complete, loved, secure, and all my needs will be met with ease and flow, including those emotional yearnings for collaboration, companionship, and co-creation.

Turn on the inner light to see the truth of life as it unfolds around you. This gift of insight, perception, and clairvoyance will activate in full. Now is the time the entire universe is organized. All your healer, guides, helpers, teachers, mother, father, God, higher self, and the Emissaries and all light beings are here to amplify your ability to see the truth, the true essence in yourself and all things. We are the Emissaries of the Third Ray, the second octave of love.

❖ ❖ ❖

Sensing a deeper truth in all things was a real eye-opener for me and now is my top priority. When I first started my path as an intuitive guide was that I assumed life would be easier the more intuitive I was. I assumed I would be spared difficulties. That turned out to be slightly inaccurate. Yes, of course, my guidance prevented mistakes and led me to incredible opportunities. But I still had personal soul lessons to face (many of which I've shared with you), and I needed to dig deep and get honest about my own ego limitations, attachments, and fears. I had to overcome my reactivity and avoid jumping to conclusions. I needed to learn to view life more objectively and not take people so personally as I had been. When meditating one night, it became clear to me that all life experiences occur for our soul's benefit. Every single one. The more committed to empowerment and soul mastery I was, the more soul challenges I would attract. Instead of viewing challenges as setbacks, I learned to see them as signs of progress. This forever changed my expectations and response to life. I went from a victim-y "Why is this happening to me?" outlook to a "Bring it on. I'm ready to grow even more" one. I embraced these psychic sit-ups and emotional workouts to grow and get stronger, to be more masterful in life. I accepted my challenges as bearers of gifts. I learned to be resilient, to manifest, to forgive, to be courageous, to get stronger, to develop my humor and creativity, to pivot when necessary, to be generous, to ask for more. I came to see most of my difficulties were of my own making. I was the Wizard behind the curtain in my private version of *The Wizard of Oz*. My life's challenges were my invention and no one else's. This was the most eye opening "aha" of all.

Still, the blessings outweighed the pain. I learned to be adventurous, take risks, and fearlessly travel the world. I learned to recognize miracles as they happened. No challenge was greater than my ability to overcome it. In each problem, I found an opportunity to grow, to be a magician, to create something new.

I shared this with a client, Daisy, who had a particularly sad challenge. She was a woman, who, since she was eight years old, had lost all her hair. She had complete alopecia. Daisy wore wigs her whole life and suffered with so much shame and pain because of it. She had seen every doctor, healer, holy roller, magician, and more, the world over, and still had no hair. When we met, she took off her wig while talking to me and said, "How do you see the truth and soul growth in this?" I could appreciate that being bald would be a tough thing to face. But I said, "What I see is not important. What truth do you see? Answer intuitively, and not from your angry ego. What are you seeing and not seeing here?" She said, "What I'm not seeing is my beauty. I don't see beauty in me at all. I'm ugly. I'm shameful. I'm not feminine. That's the truth." She was defiant when she said this, and it was tough to hear. I knew she fully felt it. Certainly, the outer world confirmed much of what Daisy felt about herself. I replied, "It's subjective. I find you beautiful and heroic. Maybe that's what you are here to discover. Maybe it's not about your hair or your body or any other external attribute. Maybe your soul wants you to see the beauty in you and evolve your perception of beauty. Maybe. I don't know."

Daisy wasn't available to hear this at that moment. But later, fed up with the stress of hiding her condition, she decided to throw away her wigs. She was tired of hiding, hoping no one saw how ugly she was. She said, "I no longer care if I'm beautiful or not. I'm done trying to convince others to see me as beautiful when I don't see it myself." I was so happy to hear she gave up the wigs I nearly cried. She was willing to see a new truth. That decision took courage. Our conversation took place five years ago.

The last time I saw Daisy, I was shocked. She had a beautiful head of dark-black hair. I said, "Daisy, my goodness. What did you do?" And she said, "I stopped hiding. Two years later, my hair grew back. I decided I wasn't going to define myself in this superficial way as you suggested and stopped. It was not easy at first but got easier fast. I never encountered meanness in the outer world or heard anyone call me ugly. Nobody said a thing to me. I also noticed a lot of bald people, men and women alike, and a few suffering from chemo. They were choosing baldness as a fashion statement. Then, my hair grew back."

"That's really impressive, Daisy," I replied, awestruck. "Today, I am learning from you," I spoke. "Besides, you've proven that we are all beautiful spiritual beings. It's just up to us to see it."

What truth are you becoming aware of today? What truth might you be denying? Be curious when contemplating this question. Be playful even. Ask your spirit, "What's the truth of anything? What truth am I missing?" If you are sincere, it will pop out at you when you least expect it. Trust me. We are awakening. We are not to feel as though we are looking for a needle in a haystack anymore. Our spirits are collectively evolving at lightning speed. So, the truth of our divine nature becomes quite strong as we move forward. In truth, we are the Emissaries of the Third Ray.

LESSON 13

CHOOSE WITH LOVE

Dear one, are you experiencing so many transformational shifts that sometimes it feels a bit overwhelming? Have you noticed your body changing or feeling off balance or ungrounded? At the same time, are things unfolding in a new, exciting way? Both your physical body and the physical Earth are changing, and adjustments need to be made to stay grounded. You are increasing the amount of energy and vibrational frequency your physical body uses every day and which you express.

The same is happening in your physical body and in your consciousness as you evolve. You are moving dense energies out and brighter, higher energies in. This is creating a temporary collision of energies. Do not fear the physical disturbances that may come and go, such as bouts of vertigo, buzzing in the ear, awakening in the middle of the night, extreme fatigue, and more. Your body is adjusting to a higher frequency, and these disturbances will subside in time. Here are two suggestions to help move through this adjustment phase quickly.

The first is to be grounded. As an energetic being in a physical vessel, it is important to understand the needs of the physical vessel during this transformation period, so that you make choices that support a heightened frequency.

For example, you may suddenly no longer tolerate noisy atmospheres or no longer desire food or drink that leaves a heavy or toxic aftereffect. You may no longer be interested in mind-numbing activities such as scrolling on a phone or playing video games, preferring meditation, quiet, and sleep instead of adjusting to these higher frequencies. You may prefer to maintain peace and quiet and time in nature.

Secondly, pay attention to what you eat and how it, too, affects you. Choose foods that leave you feeling well-nourished and relaxed. Be mindful of the amounts of food you consume at one time, selecting lighter portions, eating more frequently. Avoid processed foods far removed from their source, from nature. These do not support a higher frequency. There are no specific rules to follow. Choose what feels supportive to you. If you drink alcohol, for example, notice how it affects you. If you notice no shift in vibration, then this is acceptable to your physical vehicle. But if you have a negative reaction to such ingestion, such as irritability, depression, exhaustion, anxiety, insecurity, or more, then this is not in alignment with your vessel and should be avoided.

Drink water to raise your vibration to a much higher level. We suggest you hydrate frequently and regularly. Water is not available to everyone on Earth. It is a great gift if it is available to you. Water keeps your body grounded, your emotions clear, and your intuitive faculties functioning well.

Beyond physical considerations, respond to life with love. Nourish yourself with love. Meet every circumstance, however challenging, with love. The challenges will decrease with love, not with fear, not with judgment, not with resentment, not with competitiveness. Love takes care of you. The more loving you choose to be, the more self-loving, other loving, responding to all with love, the more empowered you will be. Avoid being trapped by hateful energy, as it will want to pull you in. It's easy to fall into hateful energy. "I hate what is happening. I hate the leaders. I hate the injustice. I hate my body." Hate nothing. Anytime hate comes through you, you lose power.

This is not to suggest you fall in love with what is unacceptable to your divine spirit and your sense of love, justice, and harmony. If something offends you, step away. Say aloud, "I release this; I do not accept this. I release myself in love. I choose love."

Your choices in matters of body, mind, and spirit are important. Making conscious and healthful choices is not easy. It takes consideration and discipline. Following these laws lays the foundation for soul mastery. They take practice. They take attention. Choose what soothes your emotions, and avoid that which disturbs your spirit. This is not to deny grief, pain, and suffering. They're a natural part of the human emotional experience, but hatred is not. Hatred is the distorted outlook of a fearful ego. It serves nothing and is poisonous to your spirit. When you feel reactive, summon love. Ask for help from the universe for love and neutrality to soothe when you need it. Invoke love. This is the law. We are the Emissaries of the Third Ray, the second octave of love.

This law is challenging to the ego, isn't it? It is difficult to love when chaos breaks lose. I have dear friends in Morocco who went through a terrifically upsetting earthquake recently. Nobody died, thank goodness, but the homes were destroyed. It brought about terrible suffering, and anger too, especially toward building planners who ignored building codes, putting people in the grave danger they just experienced. My friends were consumed with hatred over this. But it made things worse. I tried my best to stay in love rather than hatred, but their energy was so overwhelming that it wasn't easy. Showing up in love to people who are suffering requires determination. This comes with spiritual practice. Being loving starts with breathing. Breathing brings you back to your heart. Breathe before solving problems. Breathe before judging and reacting to people and situations. Breathe before taking any actions. Breathe as a co-creator and not a victim. Breathe before asking, "What can I lovingly do to help?"

Recently a friend who was visiting Paris was walking home, having just spent the most gorgeous time of her life just basking in the summer evening. Eventually she wandered in front of a major department store across the street from one of the public buildings where she saw several women and tiny babies camping on the street right there. This shocked and traumatized her and seemed so out of place against this gorgeous backdrop. This group of vulnerable women and children shattered the illusion of her perfect summer night in Paris. These desperate women and children sitting on cardboard slabs enraged her. "Why are they here?" she wondered. They looked so desperate, and there was no one around to give her any insight as to what she was witnessing. When we spoke the following morning, she was still so upset. She even looked into the situation further, needing to know what was going on. Why were they there? She learned this spot was an agreed-upon location where these women and infants could get help, where the locals knew to arrive and offer them shelter, give their babies food, diapers, even a place to spend the night. She investigated their funding, inquired about the sources they drew from, and asked how she could help.

She discovered several organizations raising money for these women and babies. Seeing these suffering women and children affected her so deeply, she immediately joined one of these organizations. What started out to be a fun summer vacation led her to her purpose, pointing her in the direction to do something for others, a need she had but had not consciously acknowledged. This vignette shows the law of love in action. We can react and be appalled by others' pain, but that doesn't ease what we witness. Responding with love can.

Love in action helps heal people. How many times do we hear and see world tragedies, and in response send prayers of love and light? That helps some, but loving actions help more.

This particular law asks us to recognize our connection to one another and invites us to engage in loving actions wherever possible, and especially when connecting with our fellow humans. Our world is struggling in so many ways. We cannot do everything to ease pain and suffering we witness, but we can always do something, and especially something with love. Even a small loving act, such as acknowledging someone's presence by looking them in the eye and smiling, can have a lasting positive impact on everyone. The Emissaries share this law to invite us to act with love wherever we are, with whomever we are with, and in whatever situation we are in. The divine law is clear. Act with love.

If there is something in your world that offends you, something that appalls you or scares you, like the climate or the government or wars or homelessness, do you respond in a loving way, adding to the healing, or do you react, thus adding to the pain? Even one loving action toward anything that needs love helps tremendously. Check in to see if you are loving yourself first. When you love yourself, loving others comes more easily. Attend to your priorities, attend to your work, be present to your people, then contribute to the greater community, one loving action at a time. All loving actions matter. This is the divine law.

LESSON 14

ENDINGS AND BEGINNINGS

Welcome, dear one. Your soul is here to learn to create. You chose to be here at this meaningful transformational time because you have both the desire to grow in your own evolution, as well as assist in the evolution of the planet, to bring in the new Earth. You are not a powerless bystander in the chaotic world. You are here as a divine being, a leader of love and light. Some of you know this. Awe wants all of you to know this. We are so happy you are here.

The journey on this plane is temporary. That is the divine law. When you acknowledge and accept that your journey through the human experience is temporary, you will be peaceful and empowered. Your soul never intended to be here permanently. As a light being, you are here to create and release. The nature of creation on Earth is always temporary, but life is eternal. Just as you observe in nature the new buds of spring in the dormant, quiet fields of winter, life is forever. Life unfolds as a cycle of endings and new beginnings, accepting and releasing. Now, you are at the ending of the third-dimension experience and at the beginning of the fourth and fifth dimensions' aspects of you. You are uniting with your divine nature, simultaneously undergoing death and birth. Every human experiences the same. This is the divine law.

The third dimension has refused to acknowledge the divinity and the eternity of the soul. The reason the third dimension is so fearful is because the ego fights and struggles to avoid the inevitable liberation of the soul through death. Humans enter physical form to experience being a creator, not to hold on to the creations; accepting endings and beginnings that come with being human makes your life experience far less threatening, far less oppressive, far more enriched. It allows you to be more present, take more joy in the moment, and be less fearful of loss, knowing that every moment gives way to the next and nothing is lost, only changed. By accepting endings, you will enjoy far more new beginnings. You will enjoy infinite life in spirit.

Do not be impatient with your emotional responses. Endings bring with them grief. It is part of the holy process to accept that you can be at the same time grieving and mourning on the subjective emotional realm while celebrating and feeling expansive in the new version of life that is arising at the same time. Presently, great transformations are occurring on Earth; much change is happening, accompanied by loss and death, but the death you witness is only death to the temporary outer form. It is a liberation from the human form. This is not a tragedy, because all souls are eternal. But it leaves one shattered if they are unaware of the eternity of the soul. Births and deaths occur all the time. Humans birth new ideas while letting old ways die. The more readily humans flow with this, the lighter and more blessed your lives will be. Deaths occur on many levels. These endings need to occur for new light to come in.

We invite you to reflect on what is ready to die in your life. What might you be holding on to that no longer has purpose, would best be liberated? What burden of the soul is asking for release? It can be a relationship that no longer serves you. It can be an attachment to a job that no longer fulfills you that is asking. Release can even be from the physical body if that is the case. Behind all release is new form, new life, new expression.

Endings and Beginnings

Embrace your eternal self, and you will enjoy life more. Let go of attachments rooted in the third dimension, including the habit of fear. Know all is well. All is safe and grounded. Fear subsides as you let go and ascend to the fifth dimension. In this dimension, you immediately experience unconditional, eternal love. Your clairvoyant, intuitive higher faculties activate fully so you directly sense the spirit within. In this dimension, you reconnect with loved ones no longer in physical form. You connect with their spirit. In this dimension, you understand why things are temporary, why the ego suffers. In the fifth dimension, you accept endings and new beginnings as a natural part of the human journey. Release the tension, pain, and sorrow that comes from holding on to what seeks to be released. Release what no longer feels right and embrace what does, what is entering, matching the vibration and expression of who you are becoming. This is the divine law. We are the Emissaries of the Third Ray, the second octave of love.

Given what's been going on on our planet for the last few years, I don't know anybody who can't sense the necessity of accepting endings and change, because there is so much of it happening in our world. We are being reminded of this divine law on a mass level. If we accept all endings as part of the natural plan, we know every ending brings us to a new and better beginning, and life on Earth becomes much easier to navigate.

I have a client, Jill, whose daughter, Julie, passed away suddenly years ago in a car accident at age 14. She was on her way home from a volleyball game after school when it happened. Julie was her only daughter, and this was an excruciatingly painful loss for Jill. She just couldn't believe it and couldn't accept it. I understood. It was unimaginably difficult to accept. Jill was clearly a student in this lesson because she wanted to die as well but couldn't.

After two and a half years of grieving, emotionally exhausted, Jill finally said, "I have to accept Julie is gone. I don't know how, but I have to release her." I suggested Jill ask her higher self; ask the spirit of Julie, her daughter; and ask her healers and guides for help. I said, "You don't have to do this alone. Ask for all the divine help available." "I can do that," Jill replied thoughtfully. "I thought she and my guides were gone." I reminded her that Julie transitioned to a different vibration, but she was never gone. "She's just not available in the way you knew." Julie's struggle continued, but she did enroll in a post-traumatic stress disorder treatment and received massage therapy, which helped unwind her body. She also started getting some support in a group. One night Jill dreamt Julie was sitting on her bed saying, "Mom, Mom, I'm so happy." Julie said, "It was so real that I felt her presence, and I knew it was true. I also knew she was present, so I started to heal. I miss her terribly, but I also feel her all the time. On one hand, she's not here, but on another hand, she's in my heart, and that's how it goes."

Accepting endings, including death, is one of the most difficult laws for us all to learn. However, the physical dimension is not the only dimension of our existence. Fortunately, in this great transformation time, we are starting to spontaneously participate more actively in other dimensions. This helps us accept the gift of new beginnings and the blessing of endings. We are now participating more actively in the spirit dimensions of who we are. In these higher planes we get to connect with our beloved ones who've crossed over and transitioned into spirit. We are able to engage, experience, communicate, and interact with our spirit guides and meet our higher selves. We experience ourselves as light beings. We enter the beauty of the divine realms. The more we breathe, relax, are present, and enjoy life, the more readily we access these higher dimensions of our spirit.

If you're struggling with loss (and I don't know who isn't), pray for help, pray for guidance, pray for support, pray for protection, pray for whatever you need to find relief. Ask in whatever way feels right for you for assistance and healing. Expect your prayers will be answered. Engage your imagination to experience yourself in spirit. This is what new beginnings and endings allow.

Endings can be a shock, but they don't have to be final. I lost my mom during COVID. I didn't get to say good-bye, as I was in Paris, and she was in Denver. But still, I sense her with me every day. I feel her presence all the time. I feel her spirit in the room and at times with other friends who have crossed over. They are all here. They come; they go. We are multidimensional beings, and many of us are now having multidimensional experiences with multidimensional beings. They are becoming for many quite normal. They can be part of your new normal too when you accept the eternity of the soul. Instead of fearing death, embrace eternal life. This will bring you peace. This is the divine law.

Choose New Behaviors

It's time to review the second set of laws of mastery: Take care of your body. See past appearances. Follow your vibrations. Trust your intuition. Don't hold on to anything.

This might seem like a lot, but because we are all growing at such a fast rate that you may already be implementing these laws into your life. You may already be meditating. You may already be seeking quiet moments. You may already have started seeing the gifts of life. Still, if these laws suggest a brand-new way to live, then perhaps you're a student. It is a great time to start. You wouldn't be available to these laws if you weren't ready to learn. Know you have divine support. Ask for it. Look around and notice where there is support. Your helpers, guides, teachers, and more are here to help you thoroughly and quickly learn these laws.

If some of these laws are familiar—some you know more than others, some you are practicing implementing into life, but you're still learning, gathering new information, opening your mind—then you are an apprentice. If you are an apprentice, carry on. Look for examples. Look for teachers. Practice. Keep learning; keep studying. Keep filling yourself with more affirmation of your light body.

Perhaps you already know and accept these laws. Perhaps you completely accept learning these laws are your purpose. If you read and say, "This is my way; this is my path. I need to really practice this," then you're a journeyman. You are learning by doing. Be patient. Enjoy. Avoid competition. Keep your focus on you. Your growth. Your intentions. Approach these laws with love. Stay grounded. And if you gravitate back to the third dimension, forgive yourself. You are learning. Growth from one dimension to another is an up and down messy process. You'll find your rhythm and your way. We all will; we are all learning. So be proud of your progress and be encouraged that you are learning. Your growth is our growth. We are in this together.

If you feel like, "I do know this. I am grounded. I do love myself. I am committed. I do meditate. I do see past appearances," then Hallelujah! You are mastering these laws, which means you are now a teacher and guide for others. The more teachers we have, the quicker the planet will rise. You are helping others just by virtue of how you live your life. Because we are all interacting on an energetic level, and we are all affecting one another; you are inspiring us. We're all in this evolutionary shift together. No matter where you are, you are evolving. You might be masterful in one law. With another, you might be a beginning student. Or you might find yourself somewhere in the middle of this learning process. This is how the learning process works, for all of us. Just be accepting and stay focused on one day at a time. Start with the first divine law. Set your focus and intention to live in this higher, new human, new Earth, and everything will fall into place.

Most of all, notice how you are gently transforming. Each of us grows in our own way, our own rhythm. We all find our flow. Soul growth is not mental; it's energetic; it's embodied. Soul growth brings a feeling of magic and joy with it. Not all the time. But when you least expect it. Not every aspect of growth is pleasant. But all usher in profound enthusiasm and optimism. Notice how your light is emerging. It is a reminder that life is good no matter what is happening. Life lessons bring with them so many different experiences; some are painful, some difficult, some frightening, shocking, wild, even thrilling. We need them all. We cannot evolve by understanding the laws on an intellectual level alone. We must live them through our feeling body, our bones and blood. Notice how these laws invite you to dive deep into your soul and advise you if something feels right, feels true, feels good to listen to. Your feeling sense is your truth barometer. It is your most accurate guide in life. Activating and following this inner light is a big part of what we are here to do. And to use this light to make the planet a brighter, more beautiful living being. The divine laws empower us, which is what we've come to experience. We're here right now because we promised ourselves and one another that we would be part of ushering in the new Earth. We agreed to step into our full light being-ness, our full divinity, and restore this Earth to a place of peace and beauty. We are learning and sharing and teaching one another the new behaviors of love and light. We are making big changes and witnessing much healing too. Onward we go. To the new you and the new Earth.

LESSON 15

MEET LIFE WITH GRACE

Welcome, dear one. Humanity is now in a moment when everyone is being asked to meet life and one another in a higher, more loving way. The old, conditioned way on this planet has been to battle in the third dimension, struggle for power, seek to control one another and the planet, and suffer terribly.

When humans justify attacking one another as they have, they do not realize the harm they cause themselves. As human consciousness elevates to a higher frequency, and new centers of consciousness in the heart are activated, and all feel their intrinsic connection to one another, the desire to harm, attack, even defend no longer makes sense or will be appealing. As you open up your higher conscious centers and experience the connection you share with all humanity, you soften the defenses that leave you numb, disconnected, and isolated. You reconnect with life, with others, and with your divine nature. This awakening is now occurring. Are you feeling this awakening in your heart?

As you raise your vibration, you raise your sensitivity to one another and increase your awareness of how you affect one another. You recognize how all humans face the same fundamental challenges for survival and have the same basic emotional needs for love, connection, meaning, security, and support. Your higher self clearly sees how some among you meet life's challenges more successfully than others. Your compassion increases for those who are struggling as the heart opens, and love flows where indifference *existed before. Leaving the third dimension and entering the fourth dimension opens the mind, and you become aware of yourself as a light being, returning to spirit. This is happening to more and more among you. We thank the forces of love and the Great Creator for this shift. Entering the fifth dimension occurs through the opening of the heart. This dimension is that of unconditional love. One of its extensions is grace, divine loving acceptance, and support. Grace is a fuel to help humanity grow.*

To accelerate your growth, we encourage you to meet life with grace. Grace is divine support. No longer meeting life from the subjective and isolated third-dimension frequency of ego and fear, you meet life with grace, which is the blessing of universal love and support. Grace brings strength and calm. Grace eases fear and softens harshness. Grace is relaxed, secure, confident, patient, forgiving, accepting, understanding, easy, loving. Meeting life with grace allows you to take nothing and interpret nothing personally. Grace opens the way for nonjudgmental, nonsubjective engagement. Grace moves you beyond any subjective and fragile ego state. Grace gives you the strength to remain grounded and feel secure, harmonious, and connected to the spirit. When you meet life with grace, you feel compassion and love for those who struggle and suffer.

When meeting life with grace, you take no offense at others' behavior. Grace frees you of judgment, fills you with acceptance, tolerance, neutrality, and humor. Grace instills generosity of spirit and the desire to understand others. Grace invites you to leave the battleground of conflict and replace it with cooperation. When filled with grace, your true, authentic spirit takes over. When you meet life with grace, you create the best possible experiences for yourself and others. No matter what is happening in your life, no matter what challenges you face, no matter what event, now or in the past, has or is unfolding, if you meet it with grace, you will receive the support and strength to get through it. Grace brings the means to fulfill humanity's highest purpose for being here.

Living with grace is a departure from what most of you are accustomed to, from what has been modeled for you. Living with grace requires intention, acceptance, and effort. It means leaving your heart open so you receive the love and support of the higher realms.

Do you wonder what life might be like if you met it gracefully, if you used the power of intention and imagination to call grace forward? Can you imagine how your life would transform, what would be different if grace healed the wounds of the past, if grace freed you from seeking approval, if grace protected you from harm? We offer you grace, but it requires a willingness to have an open heart to receive it. This may feel as though we are suggesting that you make yourself vulnerable to danger. Not at all. When in grace, you are protected from danger. The divine spirit is aligned with your Great Creator, so there is nothing to fear.

Accessing grace is a simple matter of placing your hand on your heart and breathing. The breath is the bridge between the physical and the spiritual realms. Breathe into the heart and exhale, releasing all the troubles you face. Breathe into the heart and ask your heart to open. Allow us to flood your heart with love and strength, with grounded calm neutrality, with grace. Open to this experience at your own pace. Notice the effect grace has on you. Sense the differences in vibration: that of lower vibrations and those graced in the higher frequencies, the fourth and fifth dimensions. It will become very quickly evident that meeting life with grace, with an open heart, and with nonpersonal awareness, brings you peace. This is the divine law. We are the Emissaries of the Third Ray, the second octave of love.

Meeting life with grace has been, in the past, one of the more challenging laws for me. I grew up in a family with three older brothers who bullied and beat me up regularly (playfully, of course), but still, it taught me at a very young age to be prepared for a fight. And yet my experience throughout life has shown me that fighting isn't going to get me anything good, because even if I win, I lose. Fighting never rewards. The laws of grace asking us to not take people's behaviors personally have been my salvation. Grace brings me peace. I treasure this peace now and will fight for my peace instead of fighting with others.

Remaining peaceful in the face of provocation is not easy, and something I've not been able to do alone. I need divine support to help me remain calm, neutral, and nonreactive in life. I am an emotional being. I get triggered if I'm not grounded and centered in my heart. Asking for divine grace has made it possible for me to stay present and calm. Receiving grace has afforded me the ability to be nonreactive and stable when I could otherwise become combative or get upset. I've learned to make myself available to grace with daily mental and emotional calming practices: meditation, solitude, contemplation, uplifting and beautiful imagining, breathing, prioritizing what brings me joy, cultivating a sense of humor, prayer, and accepting rather than reacting to others. The alternative was to be constantly triggered and distressed at my inability to control the world. These practices give me the ability to receive grace. These are my core values. I practice them daily. Without these practices, I doubt I would be grace-filled at all. I'm sure I would not. I would be a reactive, distressed, combative, miserable, and fearful mess. And I wouldn't like myself or my life much either.

The greatest gift that comes from meeting life with grace is that it creates a drama-free zone. Which is a beautiful relief.

I grew up in a big, loud Romanian family where drama was part of our entertainment. Creating a drama-free zone took me a while. I had to get used to it. My nervous system was addicted to the excitement of drama. I looked for the adrenaline drama created. Thankfully, I've weaned off drama and love the peace. I'm mindful of the requirements that calling grace into your life presents. You have to wean off the intensity and train your nervous system to relax as I did.

I have a client, John, a wonderful man and a devoted spiritual practitioner who consciously creates his life as he chooses. John is married to a lovely woman, Ellen, and they have three children, ages 11, 9, and 7. John and Ellen shared a wonderful life until Ellen turned 47. Then, all of a sudden, Ellen started behaving very oddly, so differently from what he had known. His loving wife, devoted mother, good friend, easygoing Ellen started to change after the death of her father. Suddenly, Ellen began behaving in erratic ways. She started going out at night, lying, then having affairs. Every bit of trust that they had built over the years of their marriage was shattered. Ellen asked for a divorce, abandoned her kids, and left without a bit of remorse. John could not understand what the heck was going on with Ellen when we spoke. He said, "I'm not meeting life with grace at all. I am angry. I want to punish her. She's so hurtful. What's she doing? She's out of her mind!" Everybody he knew shared his opinion and supported his fury. His friends and family told him to divorce her, punish her, not give her access to the children, and righteously so. All these third-dimension justifications made sense, but in his heart, John didn't feel this was the correct response to all this chaos. Something told him not to be victimized by her behavior and become curious instead. He prayed for grace, and during his meditation, he was guided to review her behavior from a nonpersonal standpoint. Then he was advised in spirit to ask her to check her hormones, her biology, even have her brain checked. John approached Ellen gently, in a nonaccusatory, noncombative, quiet way, and for months, he consistently asked her to do this. Eventually, Ellen agreed.

And upon closer examination, the tests revealed that, maybe from stress, trauma, or just her body being what it was—a body—Ellen had apparently suffered several ministrokes that might have affected her brain. Her doctors conjectured that this might be the root of some of her incredibly erratic behavior. The information was a shock to both John and Ellen. She was young. Why would she have a stroke? But she did. This new information changed John's outlook, helping him remain calm and find grace for Ellen's behavior and plight. John assured Ellen that he would help her, at least to recover her physical health. Over the next six months, as Ellen started getting treatment, she started to come back to her more peaceful, familiar self. John was relieved because he loved Ellen. His neutrality and grace helped restore Ellen's health and saved their marriage. A year later, Ellen moved back home, and they are now in the process of creating a new beginning.

Last I spoke to John, he said, "I am so glad I didn't take the combative path forward because I felt so hurt and betrayed. Thank goodness I didn't, because that would've only further fractured our family and negatively altered the course of all our lives, especially those of my children. It has not been easy, but we're growing; we're healing. We're deepening our sense of understanding and love—unconditional love and compassion for one another." John's story is a beautiful example of the challenge and promise of meeting life with grace. It is not easy, but from my experience, it is easier than meeting life with a fight, with drama, with reactivity that never leaves you feeling peaceful. Meeting life with grace isn't to say you should be passive. It's not inviting a lack of boundaries. It's not asking you to indulge behaviors from others that don't work for you. Not at all. It's important to maintain a sense of self-love and boundaries always. But boundaries aren't walls. Boundaries allow others in. Walls keep them out. Don't point energetic weapons toward the other either. Grace reminds us that often there is more going on than meets the eye. It also suggests you have more support to draw from in spirit than what your ego can offer.

The most important part of this law is that we can't meet life with grace on our own. We need to reconnect to our source of support to receive grace. If we open our hearts and make a connection with our creator and with the divine support we have available to us, it becomes possible to move beyond our own fear and indignation, to soften and ease our mindset, and to be open to learning why things are unfolding the way they are versus being reactive, defensive, wounded, and righteous when we are totally wrong.

Meeting life with grace brings forward a brand-new you. If you set your intention and "fake it till you make it," grace arrives. Give this a try. Ask your higher self to take over when dealing with challenges. Set the ego aside, for now. We know what that will get you. It will only exhaust you, work you up, stress you out, and worse.

Call upon grace to help you meet life's challenges. Grace gives you strength. Asking for grace has worked for me. It can work for you too. "Fake it till you make it," if you must. Grace does come to the sincere person, but it doesn't force a thing. It eases in. And when it does, it will make anything you face easier.

LESSON 16

LIVE IN INTEGRITY

Dear beloved one, we do understand most definitely the morass of colliding energies, behaviors, influences, values, intentions, and habits that you have to shuffle through and sort apart to stabilize and align yourself with the frequencies of your elevating soul and divine spirit. We understand that it is a process that requires a great deal of focus, attention, effort, introducing of new behaviors, and undoing of old programming, clearing the imprints that have been so deeply implanted in your subconscious mind. And yet the new you now must make choices that keep you in integrity and support your higher self, your divine nature, and your loving, empowered, creative spirit, rather than remain subservient to the isolated ego you, who is limited, powerless, and afraid.

The higher vibrational way is to choose to live in integrity. This means listen to your inner guidance, follow your intuitive compass, seek the highest energy and vibration, and recognize dissonance and remove yourself from it. Acknowledge incongruencies when you encounter them, and distance yourself from experiences, commitments, relationships, and entanglements that do not reflect, honor, or support your true essence and spirit. You'll meet resistance. You may be asked to justify, rationalize, or defend your new priorities. These are attempts to pull you back to the third dimension. Do not fall prey to this interference. You do not have to explain your decision to love yourself, elevate your spirit, live in alignment with your highest self, neither to others nor even to your own ego. Ignore internal or external confrontations. Live in integrity, aligned with your new soul values and priorities.

You will encounter situations that reflect old patterns of the third dimension, behaviors that have controlled you with fear and survival. The ego feels threatened by change and tries to prevent it. It prefers to keep you entrenched in the familiar even when it is of low vibration and draining to your spirit. Your ego may insist you remain in toxic relationships, remain in soul-sapping jobs, stay in the same circles with the familiar but demoralizing people, because what is predictable feels safe for the ego, even when it is prison for the spirit. Divine law asks you to live in integrity, to be at one with your spirit. This means breaking free of all conditions and connections that keep you stuck in third-dimension values, imprints, and beliefs, or surround you with people encased in limiting beliefs. We urge you, do not tolerate these incongruencies. If you feel dissonance and disturbance, then know this is not where your spirit and soul want to be. These vibrations are not in alignment with who you are becoming. They hold you back. Follow vibrations that bring you peace, ease, harmony—vibrations that lift you up. Release what is not working, and embrace the new.

Do not fear; you are never alone. You are not being led to a dead end, although it may temporarily appear so. If you are looking through the eyes of the ego, listening to your inner guidance feels uncertain, even dangerous. If you listen to your body, listen to your heart, listen to your physical experience, you will feel whole and complete. When you are disturbed in a deep way, you are out of alignment with your spirit. Correct your course, and all will be right once again. All doors will open.

This is the moment of transformation, time for committing to the new you. Be free of your ego and connect to your heart. Embrace your divine nature, and follow a higher, more loving frequency. Quiet your mind, ground your body, turn away from the noise of the world, and follow your spirit. These are the natural choices as you leave the third dimension and commune with your guardians, angels, higher self, and loving creator. Live congruently, vibrationally aligned as the light being you are. We are the Emissaries of the Third Ray, the second octave of love.

While in this great transformation time, we are all reevaluating what it means to be in integrity, to live authentically. The old way of being is to try to figure out life, cling to the familiar even when it doesn't feel right for fear of the unknown, cling to unhappiness over taking risks, play it safe, be dishonest with ourselves and others to preserve security or avoid being alone, and deny how we feel. The ego you doesn't want to take a risk for fear of being wrong, or making a mistake, so it justifies staying miserable in the wrong situations, saying, *"I have to do this. I have no choice."* You do have a choice. And yes, I appreciate very much how challenging it can be to follow your heart, when every bit of programming and external evidence tells you that if you make a change or you let go or you do something different, you are doomed. But listen, as the Emissaries suggest, to your body and heart. Ask your inner light to align you with the truth and lead you to the best opportunities and connections in the world to support your light.

This reminds me of a woman I just spoke with a few months ago whose name was Elizabeth. She had worked as a psychiatric nurse in her younger years, then took some time off to raise her family. Recently, Elizabeth decided to go back to work, but she had a difficult time finding a job. She was finally hired to work in an addiction center, helping people who were struggling with serious drug addictions and debilitating mental illnesses. Her ego rejoiced. *"This is a perfect job for me,"* she thought. *"I'm over 55, so I'm so lucky to be here, and it offers insurance, so I can't complain,"* so she told herself. Except the place was poorly managed, her co-workers were angry and unpleasant, and the hours were way too long, leaving her depleted and beat up emotionally by the time she went home, night after night, feeling miserable. Still, financial fear kept her going. *"I have to keep this job. There are no more jobs. I'm too old. I should be grateful. This is doing good things for people."* Her fearful ego kept her trying to do the "spiritual" thing and hang on. But her body was honest and rebelled. It started breaking down, first with low back pain, then sciatica; then her hip went out, then her other hip, and finally she became so entrenched in physical pain that going to and from work was pure torture.

She knew she had to quit and look for less stressful work, but her fear and stubbornness refused. "I'm in pain because I sit too long. I just need to get up and stretch," she told herself. That made logical sense, but it wasn't the truth. She didn't want to be there, and her body made that clear. When we spoke, Elizabeth admitted, "I'm terrified. I need to quit my job, but my doctor said I might need hip surgery, and if that's the case, I need the insurance to cover it for me. But I worry about the recovery because I live with my partner, and he's not well." She was backed into a corner.

I was quiet for a long time, listening to her energy, body, and spirit. Finally, I asked, "Elizabeth, what does your heart say? Because Elizabeth, I don't think you're confused. I think you're afraid to quit and hope you can use a surgery to get around it. A surgery that may not be necessary," to which Elizabeth instantly blurted out, "You are right. I have to quit this job. It's making me sick; it's hurting my body. The amount of stress it's having on me is breaking me down. Now I'm actually hoping my hip will break down so I can take a medical leave."

"I appreciate your creativity," I responded. "You're trying to find a way out without actually saying I quit." "Yes," she answered. "That is my plan. Will it work?" I said, "The problem with your plan is you might be underestimating how painful hip surgery and recovery can be. It might be less painful to start looking for another job rather than force a surgery to get out of a bad situation." Her ego kicked right back in. "Well, there's only two of us, and my partner had a stroke two weeks ago. Fortunately, he's recovering, but now he's going to be out of work for a while." I laughed, and asked, "Is that where you got the idea for the hip surgery?" She was quiet, then said, "Exactly."

"Before you have surgery, consider asking your higher self to guide you to the right place and path; ask for support to find something with the least amount of suffering and pain. I'm not saying yes or no to your plan. I suggesting you open to another way." I never heard back from Elizabeth. I hoped she found her way. Her ego would force things, but it wasn't her only option. She just had to see that for herself.

Divine laws don't force themselves upon you. You always have free will to do what you choose. It's just that when you choose fear, it follows you. It doesn't leave. If anything, problems worsen. Being honest opens the way to flow instead of backing you in the corner. The divine laws are sometimes difficult to trust, but give them a chance. Just ask yourself what is true. Is life working? Are you in the flow, or are you talking yourself into remaining in places or with people who aren't vibrationally correct for you? These aren't easy answers to hear. Most people don't want to hear them, in fact. Most of the time, the ego chooses to remain where they are miserable. If you don't want to be one those miserable people, you have to change the channel and listen to your inner voice and heart over your ego. You have to get out of your head. Breathe and focus on your heart. Be quiet. Go for a walk in nature. Be open to what your heart and spirit are telling you. And follow it.

If you truly desire to know the path of highest growth, your heart will show you, but it will likely involve letting go of the something you might be holding on to. A significant teacher once said to me, "You cannot reach out for something greater until you let go of what you're holding on to now." That's the meaning of surrender. To let go, release what isn't in vibrational harmony with your spirit, knowing that releasing is not the same as quitting. It opens for something better to come in. It will.

We are all given nonstop opportunities to grow, but we miss them if we're afraid to admit what isn't working. It might be easier letting go if you imagine the universe will meet you halfway. If you decide to let go, the universe will step in. Not the other way around. You can move this process of growth and change along by asking the universe to help you. It's far more secure to let go of the wrong thing and reach for the right one for you. It can feel like leaping into the void. I know. When I let go of my home in Chicago and moved to Paris, I felt like I was leaping into the void for sure. But everything in me said what I was moving toward was infinitely better than what I was leaving behind.

To take a leap of faith and let go of what isn't working, it is easier to try this: Start imagining making friends with the unknown, and believe the unknown comes bearing gifts. Believe the unknown is filled with love and support in every way, and that by letting go now, new and wonderful things can come in.

They did in my life, and they did in so many of the lives of my students, so many of the lives of clients I've worked with. When you let go of something that truly isn't right for you, even if that process is challenging, you will absolutely encounter something better. And it is the end of the old you. That's why it's so big. The old you that you're committed to that isn't working opens you up to the new you. So do imagine the new you making those choices. Not the old, fearful, scared, self-abusive you, the new you. The "I love myself, I love my spirit, I am loved by the universe, I am infinitely supported" new you is wanting to come in now. And if you say yes, the old you will be terrified until you get to the other side of yes and then will get on board. Your ego will start helping you. If you have a lot of pushback, just remind yourself, "This is going to be okay. This is all going to be okay. This is going to be better than where I am. And I'm moving back to a more authentic life."

Try it in little ways. If the new you says, "Turn here, you'll find a parking space," then turn. If the old you has a habit of going somewhere else, go with the new you. And here is a wonderful invitation. Use this prayer I was given as a child, and I say every day. It's very simple, but say it out loud: *Divine spirit, the highest energy and consciousness in me. Move me in the direction of my highest good this day. Get me out of my way and move me in the direction of my highest good and my greatest contribution.* And then watch—you'll start moving despite the fact that your ego's trying to hold you back.

LESSON 17

LEAD YOUR LIFE

Dear one, it is time to adopt behaviors and practices of your higher, elevated, spiritual self. A glorious human experience unfolds when your choices, your decisions arise from your inner light. Fumbling forward, pushed about by the external influences and limited, subjective, often negative and fearful feedback and perceptions of others will always lead you astray. Living in a higher dimension means assuming responsibility for your life as a divine creator. This is an empowering and liberating choice. It is not threatening as some fear it is. You are brilliantly capable to lead your life. No one is better equipped to guide you than you. Taking responsibility means embracing the ability to respond to all that presents in your life in a self-loving, creative, harmonious way. Taking responsibility for yourself as a fifth-dimension light being means accepting every circumstance, encounter, situation you find yourself in, every person you relate to as an Earth-creation-school opportunity to learn and grow. Nothing occurs in your life by accident, from the most intense experiences to the most insignificant. All that unfolds offers an opportunity for the soul. To respond to life responsibly, simply turn inward and breathe into the heart. Quiet the mind and listen within instead of soliciting input from the outside. When centered in the fifth dimension, open to the uninterrupted flow of inner guidance surging in every cell of your being. Silence the noisy chatter in your head by calmly breathing. Confidence, security, and peace naturally follow when you turn to your inner light for direction. Clarity brightens your cells. Feel this calm energy and follow its flow.

In the third dimension, many of you were taught to surrender your power to others, to seek permission from others on how to be and what to do. From the earliest age, your inner flame was extinguished, and you were thrown into darkness. You were denied the right to follow your inner guidance, trained to ask mostly less informed others to guide your way.

Now it is time to assume self-empowerment. It is time to be mindful of who and what is influencing your decisions. It is time to recognize when and how you give away your power and to whom. Still, it is natural and valuable to look for mirroring, support, affirmation, and encouragement from others. Be discerning. From whom are you soliciting such support? If you receive inner guidance to change your life but ask a fearful one without an inner light, without ability to be adaptable or who is closed to change and growth, their feedback will be useless, or worse, deter and discourage your flow.

There are many, many, many humans waking up to a higher frequency on the planet, exemplifying newly aligned behavior, seeking kinship and support in this phase of their path. If you are as well, first turn inward and contemplate your options. Self-reflect, self-examine, and take full personal responsibility for the decisions you intend to make. These are not intimidating threats. These actions serve as honest mirrors. Affirm loudly and often, "I have the ability to respond creatively to my life. I choose. I decide, and I am supported by my creator. I honor the divine law as a light being; I am in charge of me." These statements will align you with your true self. Decisions made by your true self are the best you can make.

Avoid asking for input from those who simply cannot or are ill-equipped to support you. Ignore conversations that do not reflect the higher, loving consciousness. Stay away from those who hold you back out of habit, conditioning, or even cultural influence. Your spirit is your only true authority. No one else can give you permission to be yourself. Don't let anyone take this power away either. Go within to consult with your spirit when you meet life's challenges. Breathe and open your heart. Relax, then review. Ask: "What is the lesson in this, and what is my best option for transformation? What is my best choice, my clearest response right now?" This may cause your ego, your third-dimensional self to feel anxious. The ego fears making mistakes. Breathe and assure your ego, "Everything is okay. I trust my spirit. I trust the spirit of the universe loves me. I trust my creator. I trust my higher self. I trust my heart." And then do trust. This empowering shift will realign you with your divine self. Place responsibility for yourself, for your experience, in the care and direction of your divine self and your creator instead of into the hands of others. When you do, your life flows in unimaginably beautiful and miraculous ways. To live anew, you must use the power within to lead. Have no fear. You are capable. And you are not alone. You have divine support streaming from the subtle realms. When you assume responsibility for your life, the ability to respond to life as it unfolds, your higher self takes over, and everything transforms so quickly. The best you emerges: the one you have been looking for, wanting, searching, and seeking. This is the divine law. We are the Emissaries of the Third Ray, the second octave of love.*

I have long known that following guidance and ignoring outer noise is a transformational way of living. When you listen to yourself, when you become the authority and are willing to be fully responsible for your life, everything starts to work. When you trust your inner self, it works for you. Others sense your power and will respect it. They support you fully. Having the willingness to live in alignment with your most empowered self, and taking responsibility for yourself, is a complete reversal of what most people have been taught. Not just in this lifetime, but in many lifetimes. To live with this clear integrity is uncommon. It is the way of leaders and light beings, however. It is the way to follow.

And as scary as it might initially be to your ego, leading your life actually feels refreshing. At first it will feel like a test. It is a challenge, but it's also an adventure. I have a client, William, the only son in a family business whose father had developed a successful national trucking company. It was extremely profitable, and the father and family always assumed that William would take over and run the business when the father retired. This assumption was so readily accepted that William never considered what he wanted to do, or if he even wanted to run the business. He simply followed his father's expectations from his earliest memory, accepted it as fact. And because the business provided a bountiful life, William was on board with the plan. In fact, he used to consider himself lucky when he was younger, happy not to worry about money.

"I didn't have to think about what I want to be when I grow up. Not in high school. Not in my twenties, thirties, or forties!" Because his father was in such great health, he never stopped working, so William had nothing to do. When William was well into his 50s, he still felt and acted like a child. He wasn't doing anything worthwhile. He didn't have any responsibility. He had no opportunity to lead his life because he couldn't lead a thing. He knew he had to bail on the plan. Yet, as the only son, the entire family expected him to remain on standby and eventually step in and take care of them. He knew it would be impossible. This was his first stab at integrity. When he shared his desire to change the course of his life, no family member, including his wife, supported him. "Are you crazy? Don't you dare think of anything else." This, of course, created more internal soul pressure. When we met shortly after this, he said, "I've been programmed, groomed, guilt-tripped, and seduced with money to be a puppet for my father and not myself at all," he cried. "I've hated it but didn't say no." Not taking responsibility for himself as he was intuitively guided to do, he sabotaged himself with childish behaviors instead, hoping to get fired from the role. He began drinking, doing cocaine, gambling, even womanizing, trying to escape himself and his refusal to be real. He finally hit rock bottom, trashed from his addictions and shame. It was his unconscious escape hatch. And it worked. William was eventually booted out of the family business at age 58, feeling secretly liberated. After attending rehab, William moved to another state and started working with woodcarving. He found a job at a retreat center where people came to be sober. It was a simple life, but he loved it. There was little money, but it was peaceful. He didn't yearn to escape. He looked forward to being there. He was finally in charge of his life. It took 50 years and a train wreck of mistakes for William to get to the point where he chose to live authentically, but he finally did. For him, that's all that mattered. To the soul, that is all that does matter. William had entered the fifth dimension sober, creative, living honestly, content, contributing, meditating, praying, and connecting with people who loved him for who he is. That is the divine invitation and law.

A year later, William wrote and said, "Guess what? My sister took over the business. She loves it. So, I'm now at peace in my heart." I wasn't surprised. The divine plan always works out for everyone involved, eventually. When learning the divine laws, don't expect or look for things to necessarily unfold in a neat, clean-cut, linear way as you rise to the fifth dimension. It rarely works out like that. To learn this law, ask yourself daily, "Am I honestly being myself? Am I aligned with my heart? Am I healthy? Am I at peace? Am I acting like an adult? Am I taking responsibility?" These questions are what the new Earth is asking of everyone. Be the leader of your life and lead with love, authenticity, and truth, and your example will inspire and motivate everybody around you.

The path that led William to following his inner truth and leading an authentic life was messy, painful, hurtful to himself and others, and long. It doesn't have to be this way. Yet short or long, every human will eventually encounter this law as part of Earth school and be asked to learn this lesson. How your learning process unfolds depends on your choices. If you step back a little further and study William's journey, you can see his family had a chance to grow as much as he did. It was messy, but William found his way, his father reviewed his overly selfish and controlling behaviors, and his sister was allowed to offer her talents in the business. That just shows how leading your life with your heart and being authentic, loving, at peace with yourself, and at ease contributes to everyone's betterment.

If you want to get to the truth of who you are, who you are becoming, who you want to be, ask this simple question out loud: "If I weren't afraid I would . . ." And then fill in the blank. This is a tool that my teachers gave me years ago, when I was very young, and it has always allowed my heart to tune in to what is true for me, for now, and live in integrity along the way. It's only one question away. If you want to lead your life at the highest level, you must maintain integrity and have the courage to do this. The law requests you follow your inner guidance, not your fears. Ask yourself, *If I weren't afraid, I would . . . ?*

This answer allows you to live this divine law.

LESSON 18

FREE YOUR SPIRIT

Dear one, to leave the third dimension and enter the fourth and fifth dimensions of consciousness for any sustained amount of time, stop limiting yourself or keeping your light from shining. Let the true you express itself with all your facets. There's always more in you to discover.

While it is valuable to understand what has unfolded in your life in the past—and how it has and does influence your mind, body, and spirit today, and has maybe kept your light from shining—it is even more empowering and liberating to allow a new you to emerge now. Recognizing the connection between consciousness and outcome is an essential step in your ascension to higher dimensions. Consciousness determines the dimension in which you live. Third-dimension consciousness creates struggle, stress, and survival. Fourth-dimension consciousness expands beyond the limits of the physical body and enters a more creative and unrestricted field. In this dimension, you become aware that you are a light being. Here you gather as much new information as you can to learn of your newfound self. This discovery gives rise to more freedom and power, and more creative and courageous connection with others and life. Fear subsides in the fourth dimension, and understanding and curiosity takes its place. The fourth dimension is exciting to experience, much like finding freedom after being caged in a dark prison. Possibility opens up in the fourth dimension as you consider expressing yourself in new ways, freed of the fear of judgment, driven by the desire to explore. However, while freedom, fun, and fascination are fabulous, remaining in the fourth dimension does not heal your deep-seated emotional trauma and wounds. While it's a great relief to gain some space from past wounding, deep healing begins when you enter the fifth dimension of unconditional love and light. In this dimension, you cease to be bound by the past, by time and space; cease to be motivated by power and control; cease to live fearfully or struggle with others; cease to hold yourself back; and cease to choose self-damaging thoughts, emotions, and behaviors. It becomes abundantly clear to you that the only way to live in peace is with unconditional love, first for self, then for others, then for humanity and all of life, and to freely express your soul. Lasting healing occurs with freely, fearlessly, lovingly, and creatively expressing your spirit.

Let healing be your priority. There are so many new forms of healing flooding into your conscious awareness on the planet because it is time to heal and move up. Natural remedies such as sound therapies to change your inner vibration, healing touch and body work to reorient and reprogram the cells of your body, breathwork to instill relaxation and nurturing, plant medicines from the earth to rewire your brain, chanting to restore your expression, dance and music therapy to bring joy back to your soul, and prayer and meditation to connect directly with your divine self and creator. The tremendous influx of healing energies are gifts from the healing teams in spirit to assist in restoring humans to their glorious original blueprint of beauty, joy, love, light, and grace. Allow yourself to be nourished energetically with these new healing modalities. Be like the beautiful flower in the garden turning toward the sunshine in the morning sky. We remind you that the word healing *means to become whole again. A return to wholeness occurs when you reunite with your true self, your spirit. Accept that you are a light being, a student of creative consciousness on the earth plane. Woundings are an inevitable* part of the third-dimension journey back to the light. Releasing these woundings is just as much a part of the journey, if not the most important part.

Follow your inner guidance to your path of personal healing. Listen to the impulses that lead you back to wholeness, help restore your joy, and help you shine your inner light. For some, it may be a simple impulse to go for a walk in nature, play music, and dance. For some, it may be a desire to create with your hands. Or write something. Or tell stories. Many of these impulses will be unfamiliar to the old self. Your spirit may feel the urge to dance for example, and the old you may very well push back and say, "I don't dance. It's silly." Your spirit may be encouraged to paint, and the old self will say, "I'm not an artist. What I'll create is ugly." These are not the messages of your spirit. All souls paint. All spirits dance. You may be called to travel, and the old you may say, "I don't travel; it's unsafe." But your spirit travels and has throughout many incarnations and different planetary dimensions. All souls are spirit travelers. Your soul may desire to write, but the old you may push back. "You cannot write. Nobody would want to read what you write. Who do you think you are?" Every soul has a story to tell. Every soul has wisdom to share. Every soul is a writer. As you help create a new Earth, release what is blocking your spirit light by allowing your art and creativity to flow. Reclaim your art. It is the voice of your spirit. It is calling back your fragments, the aspects of your soul that have been denied or banished.

This is how you heal. To express all of who you are today. To be a beautiful beginner.

Begin to paint, begin to write, begin to dance, begin to sing, begin to explore, and play in the new vibration. Let the new you break barriers. Be willing. Be curious. Don't paint or sing or dance for the approval of others. Do it for the joy it brings you. All soul expressions contribute to the healing and evolution and ascension of the new Earth. This is your soul's desire. Heal, be whole, be *creative, be free. This is the divine law. We are the Emissaries of the Third Ray, the second octave of love.*

This divine law invites lost parts of your spirit home. I've been working with people for over 50 years as an intuitive guide, listening as they've poured out their hearts and souls and shared their loves and secret desires. Almost all the people I've known have admitted that there was more to them than they were allowing. I've heard, "I wish I could paint. Oh, wouldn't it be fun to be able to dance?" Or "I'd love to write a book or be a musician." These yearnings are natural expressions of the spirit, cast aside, chased away, banished. Their souls were wounded when they were told, "You're not good enough for that. You don't dance. It's frivolous. You want to be a musician? Are you kidding? Get a real life. You want to design? Who do you think you are? Get a job and grow up."

That's what the limited third-dimension perspective does to the spirit. It shuts down the inner light, splinters the soul, and shatters it into fragments. The controlling ego says only certain parts of you are allowed. Sadly, those parts are usually not the parts you want to express, but the parts others want from you. If others' criticisms don't chase your spirit away, your ego does, not wanting to be vulnerable, not wanting to be a beginner in some cases. Not wanting to risk disapproval. The ego wants to be assured that you are going to be good at an expression before trying it. If this is the case, you are not seeking soul expression, you are seeking ego approval.

I was coaching an extremely talented woman, Lisa, a few days ago. She worked as an executive director of a nonprofit for 30 years and had recently quit. Given her past success, Lisa was invited to be on a lot of voluntary boards and continued to do this kind of work, but when she came to see me, she admitted, "I don't want to volunteer anymore. I'm over it." And she was. It was as if the light in her eyes had been snuffed out, the smile on her face was turned down, and her energy was near zero. She continued, "I want to paint, but I'm ashamed to say it. I feel ridiculous." I asked, "Why are you judging so harshly what sounds so fabulous and fun?" "Because"—she drew in a breath—"when I was very young, I loved painting, but when I was eight or so, my mom laughed at me and told me that I was a terrible painter. I was so humiliated." "So, you took her remark as a fact, as a mirroring of the truth of who you are?" I queried. "Yes," she said, the pain from that past moment written all over her face right before me. I wasn't going to let this be. "Let's revisit what was happening when she said that to you." I pushed further. "Do you remember anything else?" She paused, reflected, and said, "Yes. She was fighting with my dad, which they did all the time. Angry, she stormed in and saw me painting instead of cleaning the house. She told me I was a terrible painter and to knock it off and to get back to my real job cleaning the house." I said, "You certainly took that to heart, didn't you? Between your volunteer and board work, you've been metaphorically cleaning other people's houses your entire life. Now it's time to get back to painting."

She was quiet for a few minutes and then laughed and said, "You know what? You're right. I am going to get back to painting. I don't care if I'm a bad painter." "Well, that's another point," I said. "We don't just do something because we're good at it. We can pursue things that are good for us too, not just that look good to others."

What's blocking your true nature could be the silenced creative in you. Committing to healing means committing to your whole self, and if your whole self lacks creative expression, something essential is missing. One of my teachers once said, "Creativity and art give your soul a voice, and if you don't have an artistic or creative expression, your soul is silenced." Think about this. What art speaks out for your soul? Is it singing, writing, dancing, cooking, tinkering, taking photos, gardening, even fashion? Or all of the above and more? As long as it brings you joy, invites you to express yourself, have more than just one facet, and leaves you refreshed and fulfilled, it's working for you.

I met another client, Michael, who was in his late 60s, retired, and full of life. He worked in sales for 45 years, earned a nice living, and had enough money to live comfortably but modestly. He and his wife were divorced, and his kids were grown. He had a girlfriend of sorts, but it was "no big deal," as he put it, and his biggest complaint was that he was bored. I asked, "What would you love to do, Michael?" He answered without missing a beat, "I wanted to act. I've always wanted to be an actor, but it's too late. My mom discouraged me as a kid and said that wasn't realistic, so I became a salesman. Heck, I was acting half the time while being a salesman, but it worked." "Well," I said, "maybe it's time to go back to acting now. You've got nothing in your way. You don't need to act for money, but you would love the experience." He was startled by the suggestion but smiled, then said with a hopeful glint in his eye that he wouldn't even know where to start. I suggested he start by taking an improv class. He brightened. "What a good idea! I *could* do that." I told him that in improv, you get to act like yourself: your spontaneous, unscripted, natural, multifaceted, silly, spirit self. The only thing to consider when joining improv is to have the willingness to be a beginner. Then have fun." He went for it. The last I heard, Michael was still in improv. He said the class was a perfect outlet for him, and he had never been happier in his life. "I'm meeting fun people, young people. I'm not stuck in my 'old man' identity. I improv now wherever I go. I'm having a blast." Michael's improv class was healing for his soul. This is what healing means. It's when you find the way to feel whole, complete, and joyful again. Healing is recovering lost parts of you. If you feel flat, bored, uninspired, or disconnected in some way, you may need to heal as well. To help you heal, ask yourself, "If I weren't afraid, what would I love to explore?" Then do that.

One of my secret desires my entire life was to write comedies or make movies. I never pursued it for the same reasons most people ignore their creative impulses: lack of confidence and lack of support. Yet, when I moved to Paris, I really did need a healing, because my spirit felt so broken. Using my own advice, I asked myself what I would do, and making funny videos came up again. Not surprisingly, I met a group of young creatives in Paris at a dinner party soon after, and the subject of creating videos came up. The next thing I knew, we got together and started playing around with some video ideas. One time we made a two-minute unscripted video on how your guardian angel helps you. We filmed it inside and outside of my apartment and front door and put it on YouTube. It received a million views. We made a dozen more videos after that. Playing with these creatives healed my soul. Healing is a soul experience, more than any other thing. Being creative and freeing your spirit is the best healing you can experience.

When you free your spirit, other free spirits spontaneously show up in your path. I booked an appointment at a hair salon in my neighborhood that I had not been to before a few months ago. When I walked in, I wondered if I was in the right place because it looked so wild. There were paintings everywhere, including the floor. Jazz music was playing loudly in the background, and a parakeet was flying from a pillar to a post above my head. Aurelie, my hairdresser and the salon owner, introduced herself by saying, "I'm going to show you how my spirit experiences you with a dance, and then I'll do your hair." This was certainly a first, leaving me both speechless and intrigued. She then conjured up a Balinese-Japanese war dance, then asked me to take a chair and enjoy. Aurelie spoke French so fast I couldn't quite follow her, but I could tell, with all her contortions and twists, she was into having fun.

Needless to say, it was the first time I got my hair done with a dance thrown in, but I loved it. Aurelie could have shaved my head that day. It wouldn't have mattered because her spirit rejuvenated mine, and I left feeling witnessed to and beautiful and entertained and inspired because she let her true nature fly. I admired the freedom Aurelie gave herself. She was living full out. My spirit guided me to Aurelie's salon and magic shop. She revived my saggy soul that day with more than a new "hairdo" just by being her kooky self. If you have a dance in you or a poem or a painting in you waiting to be expressed, or you are called to be a sculptor or a movie maker, go for it. Allow the new you. My teacher Dr. Tully once said to me, "Never assume you know anyone and most of all yourself." This divine law says get to know yourself completely. It's healing.

LESSON 19

LIVE JOYFULLY

Dear one, we invite you to remember, recall, and allow that your true nature is joyful. Your true nature is supported and supplied with all that you need to experience your life in whatever way you choose. You imagine suffering is part of the human journey only because, from the ego's perspective, there are not cycles of birth and death, only life or annihilation. To live joyfully, you must accept that the human experience is temporary. Things grow, things die, and we have shared insights and thoughts on reclaiming that natural cycle as part of who you are; you cannot fear death if you want to live joyfully. You must accept that this is a temporary experience, but that the soul and the spirit of you live on; only the physical experience of you is shortened and temporary.

Without resistance and fear polluting and creating stress on the physical body, even that is now extending into far more years in the physical body. To live joyfully is to connect with your eternal self and realize that the human experience is Earth school, a place to learn to create, but not one where you will remain forever. You learn this lesson when you fully accept that life is temporary: You can fully accept the wide range of emotions that come when you pass from physical into spiritual form; you can fully accept that grief can coexist with joy. Sorrow can coexist with delight. The human experience is complex. The physical realm offers many different experiences, all of which bring valuable lessons. To live joyfully, you accept the more difficult passages of life. You welcome them as a natural part of the human experience.

To live joyfully as a creative being, you recognize that everything we experience as humans is important. You say, "Everything that I experience has value; everything that I encounter and I engage in is for my growth." Some of these experiences are temporary, and even the endings have value. Breathe into your body, knowing the breath of you is who you are. Everything is energy that is transmuting from one form to another. Just as you are transforming from physical matter to spiritual expression, that self is eternal. Contemplate that you are spirit. Contemplate, imagine, and wonder how your life would change if you accepted that you are an eternal spiritual being who is infinitely loved, provided with all that you need through the course of your imagination. You are free to create every experience that you want if only your imagination will allow it. Contemplate how life would be if you weren't controlled by fear of death, but rather if you came to accept it as part of your life experience on Earth. We won't glamorize it. We won't suggest there is no pain associated. The human experience involves deep love and great attachment to those you love. But if you were to accept that the transition from human form to spirit is always reliable, and that though you may not have the benefit of an immediate connection, the spirit of all is always available. This new you is not a physical, trapped embodiment. This new you is spirit operating through this temporary vehicle. Spirit is operating through everything—through trees, through plants, through creation, through imagination, through every human. Begin to see how spirit is infused in everything from the farthest star to the tiniest trinket in front of you. These are embodiments and expressions of spirit.

Observe life with awe and wonder; there are so many ways in which the spirit finds form. This will restore your joy. Admire human creativity; recognize, enjoy, and wonder in the spirit in all things. Sense the spirit of the natural world. Sit with a tree. Communicate. Go to the ocean; listen to the water. Climb the mountain;

feel the support, the immovable strength and commitment of the earth. Feel the spirit in your plants. Enjoy a morning conversation with them. They are listening. There is joy everywhere. Sense the spirit in everything at all times. We are communicating with you. Speak with spirit. Speak with us. Speak with your guardian angel. Speak with your guides. Speak with your Creator. Speak with your higher self and listen as we speak with you. Look for the spirit in all things. Acknowledge the beauty and expression of spirit. Take the filters off the fear of death, off your eyes, and see how life cannot ever be stopped.

Admire the creativity that is pouring through everything, even creativity that doesn't necessarily have optimum results. It's still creativity. Neutralize your opinions of good and bad. This is part of the third dimension. The limited world. Enter a new space, a third space where all is spirit flowing, for now, through these various forms, and it's all temporary. The great teachers have said in many forms, this too shall pass. And that is one truth to live by: Whatever you are experiencing, experience it fully present, fully interested, fully invested in the experience, for it too shall pass. It's all temporary.

Liberation is when you no longer try to hold on to everything and prevent it from changing, from growing, from shifting. Let go and allow. Let go of your identity. Let go of the roles you play. Let go of your attachments and control of others or the outer world. Let go of any effort to stop and prevent growth and change and life to flow, and your joy will return. To live life joyfully is to live life in the moment, being present and admiring and recognizing how the wheels of life turn like the seasons that come and go in the physical world. There are emotional seasons; there are mental seasons; there are seasons in your own body as well that come and go and renew.

Live life joyfully, not attaching to your identity, to your personality. Ask instead, "Who will I be today? What will I allow today?" Notice where you block yourself in. "I won't follow that spontaneity. I won't make room for that." Do not ignore the voice from the soul that says, "Let's move. Let's travel. Let's meet new people. Let's rest. Let's just be." This is the foundation of joyful living. If you want to elevate your human experience, make it a joyful one. Change your identity from matter to spirit. Change your requirements from attachment to release. Change your perspective from fear to curiosity.

Let yourself be present. Let yourself be free. Let yourself explore adventure, and most of all, let yourself love. To live joyfully is to live with love, to let love be your motivation, your view, your priority. Let love be the gold you seek. Let love be your treasure. Not love from others, but love flowing through you to others and then happily letting it flow back. Because in the spirit of all things, it's true. Nature is love. When you connect to the flow of joyful love, you connect to the abundance of the universe. Every part of your life that is lacking is lacking because it is lacking in love. Living joyfully releases this lack and turns it into flow, into abundance, whether it's an abundance of material goods, money, love, relationships, affection, or good health. It is all, at its essence, an abundance of love flowing through you. Make choices that activate this loving nature, this feeling, this experience. Start every morning inviting love to move you through the day and inviting your awareness to receive love wherever it comes gracefully, openheartedly, and with gratitude. We are the Emissaries of the Third Ray, the second octave of love.

All these beautiful assists that the Emissaries are giving us are so helpful in how we learn to be our new self, our new you, our new being. But the most important one is this one. Living joyfully is a radical departure from how we've been taught to live in the third dimension. Shame, guilt, despair, fear, trauma, power, addiction, control, on and on were preferred priorities. There's no joy in those, of course, but you came in joyful. The spirit is joyful, and it's a state of being we have to choose. If we choose to have joyful experiences, remember that life is temporary and we are just going to go for it, then joy arrives.

A couple of years ago, one of my clients scheduled an intuitive reading. I work by phone, so I never actually put my eyes on her. When we spoke, she said, "I have terminal breast cancer, and I am dying. I'm not calling you to save my life. I am deeply conflicted, however, and I need your help so that I can die in peace." As I listened to her, she continued, "Sonia, I was the role-model female. I was a good student. I was a good girl. I was helpful at home. I got married young. I was a devoted mother. I served on the PTA; I organized the block parties. I did everything expected of me and was told I was a good woman, good person, good mother, good everything. Now I'm in hospice, and so many people are coming to me, all saying how good I was, and how much they appreciated my goodness. The truth is, I want to scream at them that all of that was fake, that it wasn't goodness motivated by love. It was me motivated by fear and a deep and desperate need for approval. What I want to say is, don't follow my example, because I didn't live my life at all." She continued, "I wanted to be a painter, and I never even gave myself a box of crayons. I wanted to go on trips and have fun, but I was too dutiful and responsible to ever leave my post. I was burdened with such a sense of duty for others, I never even allowed myself to go out for fun. My husband invited me to go to Europe for our 25th anniversary, and I said I couldn't because I had to do the PTA fundraiser. We never went, and now I'm dying, and everybody's congratulating me on what a wonderful person I am when I wasn't at all that inside. I was angry. I was trapped. I was like a robot. How do I die in peace?"

All I was guided to say was, "Tell everybody the truth when they congratulate you on being so wonderful. Yes, you were wonderful to them, but not to yourself. Tell them that that's the wisdom you are taking with you as you pass from this human experience to spirit. Share what you have learned as you bring this journey to a close."

She was satisfied with that, saying, "Thank you." I knew her days were very numbered. I didn't hear from her again, but many months later, her eldest daughter called me and said, "I'm not calling for a reading. I'm calling to thank you. I don't know what you said with my mom, but she became someone else before she died. She was chatty. She told us what she had really wanted to do. We brought her paints to hospice. She told everybody what she really thought. She became a person I did not recognize, but I loved. She was funny, sassy, and playful. She died happy. I never knew my mom to be happy one day of my life, but I saw her die happy."

I was so grateful she chose to end her life joyfully. The Emissaries are giving us a huge assist here in how to make our lives feel fulfilling. The number one question that I get asked by clients when they come for readings is: "What's my purpose in life? I know I'm meant for something. I'm meant to do something for humanity. I'm meant to serve in some way." The problem is, in the third dimension, we've been given models of service that are steeped in self-sacrifice, self-denial, and saving others instead of feeling worthy ourselves. So, the motive is noble, but the model has to go. My teacher Dr. Tully said to me, the best thing you can do for the miserable of this world is don't be one of them. I heard that when I was 16 years old, and I loved it. "Your vibration," he said, "affects everyone. Not just you. If you're happy, everyone around you experiences that joy." I know this is true. If you ever walked into a room where someone is miserable, you could be in the

Live Joyfully

best mood, and all of a sudden, it's like someone popped your balloon, and all the joy deflated.

Recognize your influence on others. We affect one another but tend to deny or ignore this. If we want to fulfill our purpose, being joyful is one of the easiest ways to positively affect others. The best way to live joyfully is to remember that we're only here temporarily, so let's not waste time. Do what your spirit would love to do, at least some of the time; if there is a will, there is a way. Do less of what your ego wants to do. Your ego has terrible ideas. "Let's do drugs. Let's get drunk. Let's drive a thousand miles an hour. Let's gamble." That is all trying to distract from the fact that you're miserable. Do more of what your spirit wants to do. The spirit makes great suggestions. "Let's go for a walk. Let's plan a garden. Let's play music. Let's have fun. Let's just be together. Let's relax."

To live life in joy, remembering it is temporary, mirrors values of the fourth and fifth dimensions, not the third. When connected to the fifth dimension, joy naturally becomes a priority. We're not going to stop death, so let's live full out before it arrives. Notice the spirit in all people and things, and it'll start to make you smile and laugh. It'll bring your joy back because the spirit is love. Live your life with more love. Not guilt, not shame, and not needing explanations. Living in joy is a great purpose in life.

LESSON 20

CREATE YOUR LIFE

Welcome, dear one. As you can see, the invitation to live your true nature is indeed not that complicated. In fact, it can be quite simple but does require full commitment. You are a co-creator with the universe. Earth is creation school. You are a divine spirit embodied. You have been trapped in a lower frequency vibration and a false self that you are now liberating yourself from. You sense and you feel the divine nature in you. Remember, you are here for one reason: to intentionally create a life you love. That is your only purpose, and that is the greatest contribution you can make to this planet: recognizing that you are love; you don't need it; you don't need to seek it and find it in others; you are a soul that is here to express it. The invitation, the behaviors that we have suggested, will bring you back again and again and again to this simple choice to create with intention. Commit to creating; enjoy creating. Take responsibility for creating. Experiment with creating a life you love. Give yourself freedom to invest, discover, experiment, adventure, to tune in to the deepest calling of a life you love.

Creating a life you love cannot be figured out. It requires trial and error. It does require experiences over intellectual projections. You won't know what you love until you experience it. Relax about the need to know the future, the need to know the outcome, the need for guarantees. Simply commit to creating through the process of following your heart, detaching from the false gods of approval, honoring the divine within you, and recognizing the divine in those around you.

This is a huge transformation, a brand-new way of being. It takes attention; it takes practice. Only your experiences and results will convince you that this is the way of peace. Free your attention from all time-wasting, mind-numbing activities. Be present to your breathing. Be present to your body. Be present to your communication of the heart. Be present to the moment. Listen and be interested in life, in the world you inhabit, in the people who surrounded you, and in the energy flowing all around you. In fact, devote your attention to the guidance within, be aware of and sensitive to the support you receive, both from those around you in the physical plane and from the subtle realms. Let the past go.

This is not necessarily easy for your ego. It prefers to keep repeating things over and over again, like mental recordings—no different than recordings on a tape recorder. Turn off the tape recorder. Become aware and mindful of the world around you. If this seems overwhelming, relax and breathe. Transformation is a big shift, yet it occurs in little ways. Start today. Call to mind your priorities, and set your intentions for the day. As a divine creator, imagine how you would like things to unfold, and then expect they will. Be on guard for inner and outer sabotage and resistance. The ego doesn't like change, and neither do the people around you. Do not let your or anyone else's fears get in the way of raising your vibration and living in the grace and flow of your divine nature.

Reconnect with your body. Give it plenty of water and a good night's rest. Discipline in these areas is a powerful, self-loving choice. Ignore the temptation to be drained by distractions. Your ego will encourage you to watch one more show or scroll for another half hour on the phone; this time is better spent in quiet prayer, meditation, intuitive journaling, and communicating with your divine nature. You have a choice. Choose what supports your highest nature, not your lowest. Common sense is higher sense.

Drinking alcohol, smoking cigarettes, and eating junk food all poison the body and lower your consciousness. Loud noises, toxic low-vibration people, self-doubt, criticism, and self-rejection are all choices that are not congruent with the higher dimensions. Be honest and leave these behaviors behind. Be stronger than those old tape recordings that leave you feeling trapped in the third dimension of victimhood and worthlessness. You have the key to ascension: Simply intend to create a life you love and show up in every choice, hour by hour.

You may be asking, "What can I do right now that would help me become more aligned with my divine nature? What can I commit to in the moment that would align with what I love? How do I lead my life, one small choice at a time?" The first thing you can do is not overthink. Stay in your heart and follow your natural energetic impulses. Ask your higher self and your divine support system to lead you in the direction of your highest good. Slow down, breathe, and pay attention to the world around you and the world within you. Don't waste time overthinking or trying to figure out anything. Experiment, explore, have experiences, and then make your decisions. This is the way to learn. Fear is a part of the third dimension, and you may be acutely aware of it. Remind yourself that while you feel fear, you are not in danger. You are safe, and you are protected when living in your light body and following your heart, especially when taking full responsibility for yourself. The time is now to intend to create a life you love. Commit. Be consistent. Be patient.

The physical vibration of the universe operates at a slower rate than the spiritual vibration, so many of your creations may not be immediately evident in the third dimension. Do not let appearances deter or demoralize you. The light is on its way. Just as you cannot see a flower the day after you plant a seed in a garden, rest assured the flowers of intention planted today will bloom tomorrow. The third dimension is a mirror that reflects where you've placed your attention, imagination, and commitments in the past. If you do not enjoy what you are seeing, change the intention, the image, and the internal commitment. This is how you create. If you want to create a life of consistent abundance, patiently envision, feel, commit to, and choose behaviors that are abundant in nature. You cannot fail if this is your approach. Mostly, we encourage you not to abandon your ascent to higher dimensions through immaturity, distraction, and impatience that arise from the egoic mind. Discipline is important. Discipline means to learn in a consistent and grounded way. The more disciplined you are, the more quickly you will become a master creator. You are here to learn to grow in creation school. Discipline is your ticket to success.

Create a life you love, consistently. Not just in your mind, but in your behaviors, your choices, your words, your actions, even in your thoughts and emotions. Create a life you love. You are the creator. You created the life you have now. If you love the life you have now, continue doing whatever you are doing. You are following the divine law. If there are aspects that you don't love, create something new. Be prepared for the resistance of the ego and intend to overcome it. Your divine support system is at your service. The universe is at your service. You have infinite help if only you ask. We will not interfere with your life. You have free will to create any life you desire, including a life that makes you unhappy and unfulfilled. It is nevertheless your creation. Open your heart, and let love flow to you and through you, and you will create a masterpiece.

Fall in love with creating. Affirm: "I am creating a life I love. I am having a wonderful time. I am creating it first in my thoughts, then in my emotions, then with my choices; eventually, the life I'm creating internally will reveal itself externally." Affirm: "I am living the life I love in my inner world right now." Your egoic mind will say, "You're ridiculous. You're making this up. You're imagining things." Answer, "Yes, thank you. I am enjoying it. I *am having a wonderful experience creating my life. I am powerful. I am imaginative. I am a powerful creator."* This is the way to bring your new and most beautiful creations forward. Create with intention and love. First in your thought, then in your emotion, then in your imagination, followed by your choices, and with our divine assistance, it will manifest.

We simply ask, *"Are you ready to consciously, fully commit to creating a life you love?" This is why you are here. You have all the resources available to succeed, including divine support and help. Are you ready to create a life you love? Your entire universal support system is ready when you are. This is the divine law. We are the Emissaries of the Third Ray, the second octave of love.*

This divine law simply states: "Create a life you love. How willing are you to do this? Has it even crossed your mind to try?" We're certainly good at creating lives that frustrate us, creating lives that upset us, creating lives that feel like a failure. But have we even considered that creating a life we love is the most important thing we are meant to do? It's not about what other people love. Creating a life someone else loves will not make you happy. Only creating one you love will.

My spirit guides suggest checking on my attitude and altitude. My attitude is my reminder that I am a divine creator, a glorious light being in third-dimension school, on my way back home to the higher frequencies. They say, "Do not forget your true nature." Say aloud and often: "I am a creator. I'm not a victim. I'm not disempowered. I'm not trapped. I'm not stuck. I'm not being run by the tape recorder of my past. I show up consistently to create a life I love, and I show up with love. I do not create from the ego; I create with my heart, my true nature. I do not burden myself with what is not mine to carry. I do not let my ego challenge me with nonsense. I take action to create my life; I do not expect it to come without my effort. I work with divine laws." I say these affirmations when I'm in the shower. I tell myself I am soaking them in. Creating makes us happy. We humans need to create. It's not optional when it comes to inner peace.

I have a client, Josie, who married into an extremely wealthy family at a very young age. She and her husband have a gorgeous home in Utah in the mountains. They also have unlimited resources, take frequent international trips, own several brand-new cars, live on an unlimited budget for whatever, have beautiful designer clothing and jewelry, and have no material challenges or financial stress.

Initially, Josie felt like Cinderella, whose prince had come. But after four or five years of such excessive comfort, she booked an appointment with me because, she said, "I'm bored. I'm not loving my life. I need something to do, to create." I understood. Josie was right. The human spirit is unhappy if it's not creative. We are born and designed to create, not just consume. There was only one solution for Josie, and that was to begin to be creative in some meaningful way. She knew creation was the answer. Only what? "Honestly," she said, "I don't have any idea what to create. I don't need a thing, so it makes it harder to answer, because usually creativity meets some sort of need, and I don't have any." This was true. Josie had a far more difficult challenge than somebody who needed to meet some basic needs, because as the saying goes, "Necessity is the mother of invention." When you are robbed of necessity, your creativity can definitely flatten out. Some of the most unhappy clients I've worked with over the years were generally those who were the most materially secure. Josie was no exception.

Josie's first attempt to overcome boredom was to volunteer, but after a year of that, she quit. It just didn't capture her heart. She wasted a second year trying to figure something else out, but she had no luck. Eventually, she recognized how much she loved her garden and growing flowers. She was also spiritually inquisitive and learned about the vibrational healing powers of flowers. Josie was consumed with this new interest, and in a short time, it became her overwhelming love and passion. Josie had finally found her purpose: growing flowers and creating flower essences to help people heal their emotional bodies. She started her own local company, and while she's just beginning, it's going very well, and Josie is supremely happy. Her greatest realization over the last five years was that it's far more fulfilling to create and share than to just consume. Josie's answers came from rolling up her sleeves and putting her hands in the garden dirt. All her answers came, but not one of them came through figuring anything out.

I have a client, Gayle, who said, "I'm wasting my life. I don't want to work for anybody. I quit my jobs every two years. I start new things all the time and then lose interest." "What part do you consider a waste?" I asked. "Look at all the wonderful experiences you've had. And all the glorious opportunities to meet people and be creative as well. I don't consider anything you've done a waste of time." "That's not what everybody else thinks," Gayle responded. "Everybody (meaning my family), thinks I'm such a loser." She nearly cried.

I said, "Who cares what everybody thinks? Would you rather win their approval by taking a job and staying in a role that isn't you? Maybe your purpose in life this time is to have all these experiences. Maybe you are in the flow of your soul's growth, and you're not wasting a minute. It just looks different to those on the outside. I have a question. Apart from the disapproval you're getting from your parents, how unhappy are you?" Gayle answered, "Disapproval aside, I'm very happy. I love my life!" "Then you don't have a purpose-in-life problem; you have an approval problem," I pointed out. "It's important to get over disapproval so you can enjoy living your life the way you love and are. Choose between living spontaneously and creatively as you are, with a lot of variety, versus doing something predictable to get your parents' approval. Which would you rather have in the end?" Gayle took a deep breath and said, "That's not that easy to answer, but honestly, I'll never be happy doing the kinds of things they'd approve of, so I'll just have to live with this dissonance in my life." Two things were important here. The first is that Gayle was enjoying a beautiful life, showing that the purpose of her life was to discover what she liked and didn't, and this adventuring in experimentation was the way to discover this. Secondly, you can't live an authentic life and seek approval at the same time, which Gayle was painfully discovering. Some people choose approval over genuine fulfillment, but I've never met anyone who's happy with that decision. Not having the approval of your family can be difficult, but if you're genuinely happy, the family comes around eventually. If, like Gayle, this is a challenge for you, just be patient.

There is another point to be made as well. Sometimes we end up in situations or jobs that we don't love, but it doesn't mean they're all wrong. They may have something to offer, and you need them just long enough to get the gift. I say this because that happened to me. When I was 20 years old, I took a job as a flight attendant. My ego talked me into it, pointing out that it was a great way to get around the world. And it was. My ego also pointed out that the hours were right, and it really was only a part-time job, not full time, so it was also a terrific way to have enough time off to do other things, and I did. Once into the job, however, I realized I intensely disliked it. It simply wasn't for me. I was so annoyed that I told my spiritual teacher and mentor, Charlie (who was still alive at the time), how much I disliked it and felt I was meant to do "better things." I said, "I don't want to do this job. I want to be a spiritual teacher." Charlie shocked me by saying, "You have no right to be a spiritual teacher until you can do that job, or any job, with love." That really took me off guard. He continued, "You're judging left and right and being superior and being in your ego. You haven't learned a thing if you ended up there. You don't have to love the experience, but you can be loving while doing the things you need to do." He was right. I was being arrogant. Not happy with my attitude, I started going to work with the intention of doing it with love. And within two weeks, I actually started loving it. It wasn't about the job; it was about my attitude. It lacked *altitude*. I was in low vibrations. I didn't stay very long after that, but I did get gifts of great friends before I did quit. My best friend to this day I met on that job. She wasn't loving it either, but we loved each other and had tremendous fun flying together. The point of this story is, even if you don't love something, there is tremendous soul value to doing whatever you are doing with love. It adds to your purpose and brings meaning and soul growth in the end. Intentionally create a life you love, and don't get hung up on the details. Do whatever you do with love. If you do both of those things, you can't lose. That is the divine law.

LESSON 21

SHINE YOUR LIGHT

Welcome, dear one. You are a brilliant and divine being. Your essence is light. The light is the reflection of the love that you are. The brighter you shine, the brighter you love. Not only do you heal and elevate your own life, but you also become part of the new Earth, a leader into a movement, a gorgeous shift into healing this planet back to its original frequency. Shine your light by keeping your heart open, feeling our support, feeling the connection to love, to support for each other, to the planet that you have available to you.

Life may be uncertain, but your spirit is never in danger. The planet right now is undergoing unbelievable changes that frighten the ego and feel very dark, but rather than join the darkness, be a bright light, be the one who shares love, encouragement, optimism, humor. If you're not feeling these things, it's because you are resonating back in the third dimension. It happens. You'll travel up and down in frequency. If you fall into lower frequency and become enveloped with the fear and negativity that is dominating the planet at this time, go back to your heart, go back to your quiet, go back to your personal commitments to create, and you will recalibrate back to spirit.

The planet is at a tipping point, and the light will prevail. Don't wait for the light. Be the light. Don't wait for others, which the third-dimension ego itself has been taught. Others will decide for you the experience you have. Others are responsible for this planet.

Others are creating the problems. We are all connected. Do not underestimate the power of your light. Your light, if shined without limitation, if shared with love, generosity, and confidence, can light a city, and that city can then light a country and the world. If you fall into shadow, look for the light. Don't feed yourself on more shadow. Look for what is uplifting: pray, sing, use mantras, dance, create, go to the light. It will reignite your own.

If you focus on the light, you will contribute to the light. We are moving back to the light. This beautiful planet Earth, which we serve, was originally conceived in love and is returning to love. It may even seem impossible, but more light than ever is being poured into the planet now. A new Earth is being born. It is happening. You are part of it. You are part of this healing. You are part of the planet's return to peace.

The only way you can keep your own light shining, dear one, is through personal self-love; self-care; self-congruency; compassion; patience; nonjudgment; deep, loving acceptance of self, not the ego; acceptance; appreciation; connection with the spirit of you; and then the recognition that it is a shared spirit. You are part of the one spirit of love that breathes this planet into being. When you choose to be a light in the world, you have reconnected and recalibrated to your true self. You are in the fifth dimension. Life will become quite different in the most beautiful ways; things will flow. Synchronicities will occur. Your gardens and dreams will grow. Your abundance will show up. These are not false promises. These are the energetic effects of living in love and in harmony with the new Earth. The body will get stronger; the emotions will lift. If you choose to be a light in the world, your life will heal and flow, and you will become a healer. In this expression of darkness, you will relieve pain by your presence. This is a choice. The invitations, the new behaviors, the new you, are all a choice. You are ready to make that choice, but it is important to know that once the choice is made, the practice begins. Have patience, humor; observe, study, learn. Notice rather than being frustrated when you are vibrating back to the lower frequencies; there's no need to judge or be unhappy. Just study what brought you there. What influences lowered your vibration so that you can correct these choices? Avoid the circumstances; change the behavior; observe with neutrality, curiosity, compassion, and affection—a great deal of affection for you as a courageous soul committed to creation school to bring in the new Earth.

Consciously commit to what amplifies your life. Commit to what amplifies your light and allows you to live joyfully. If your mind begins to trouble you, asking for justifications, sabotaging your commitments, trying to derail you, use humor, laugh, and reassure your ego. We're okay; everything's okay. You can relax, but do not put a lot of attention on those things that block you. Keep your attention on the light. Keep your attention on the moment. When you feel overwhelmed, you have left the present moment. Come back to the present moment and look for the beautiful spirit around you. Let this be your antidote and your escape route from trapped negative energies that are tormenting you. Look for the spirit; look for the life force. Look for the divine in all things, and you will rise. You will recalibrate to the frequency of your spirit.

Have no expectation or judgment. Don't judge a day as good or bad. That is the duality of the third dimension. That is the lower frequency. It is a day. What will I create? What will I experience, and what will I learn this day? Keep it that simple. Keep it that interesting. Be that curious. What will I create? What will I learn? What will I attract this day? We do encourage exercising your imagination like muscles to fill you with beautiful images to pour into your emotions. Inspirations for joyful feelings. So much of your heaviness is simply a habit that needs to be broken and replaced with a new habit. A more uplifting, imaginative, creative, joyful habit can be developed with your intention.

You are a bright light in the universe. Turn on the bright light, and be a bright light in your human journey. Believe it; experiment. Draw your own conclusions. You'll see that the brighter you turn on and live your light, the more gorgeous and joyful your life will be. You are only a bright light in truth and essence: a beautiful, loving, bright light in the universe. We adore your bright light. It heals and ushers in the new Earth. We are the Emissaries of the Third Ray, the second octave of love.

When I was very young, I started my spiritual teaching. I had mentorships. My first teacher was my wildly creative mother, who was just absolutely untethered to any need for approval from anyone. She lived in a world that was highly creative, but believe me, it brought with it a tremendous amount of chaos and drama. But with it came freedom—freedom to just follow your spirit.

Her spirit was on fire. It wasn't calming and grounding. It was passionate and inviting, but I learned very young, from observing her, the power of turning on your light. People do nice things for you if you turn on your light. People want to be around you. You are attractive. When she was alive, my mom would always greet people saying, "Tell me something good. What's the most beautiful thing that happened to you today?" And I would see people go from ash and gray to rainbow color auras in an instant because she spoke to their spirit. She taught me not to live role to role, communicating on the third dimension of ego to ego, but to live spirit to spirit, communicating authentic self to authentic self. That is how we live our light and how we turn that light on in others; we respond very quickly to those whose light is on. We call it different things. Charisma. Charm. Mojo.

In fact, in the world of social media influencers, where there is so much emphasis placed on appearances, we see hundreds of physically gorgeous human beings, but there's no light in their eyes. So they are unmemorable. The minute you encounter someone whose light is beaming brightly from their eyes, and they have a smile radiating in their aura, you can't get enough of them. You love their energy, and within a few moments, you *resonate with that energy and channel it too.* I was with a friend recently who had just moved to Paris from Portugal, an American expat like me, and was feeling very ungrounded, which I understood. Moving from one country to the other is certainly no easy feat. One night we met for dinner at a restaurant very near my home. The place we chose was too touristy for us, really, but we both just wanted to grab a quick bite and catch up, so we went with it.

The waiter we had was so impatient. He was irritable and outrageously rude, which frustrated me because I wanted my friend to have a nice experience. When he threw the menus down at us, wanting to change the vibe, I said, "I love your hair." He did have quite an interesting braided hairdo, and I knew that he put a lot of love into it. Upon being complimented, he immediately changed his channel. "Oh, thank you." He smiled. I said, "You look beautiful. That is quite the look. It's working for you." With that, he went from being an obnoxious, impatient waiter to someone who was proud to be seen as an artist and a creator. He said, "It's what I do. I do hair." With this, our whole interaction changed.

The next thing you know, he was attending to us like we were royalty, and at the end, he gave us desserts on the house. Being a bright light in the world is a very self-interested choice because your bright light is infectious, and using it can be entertaining. You can even make it a game to turn your light on with others. Watch how your light turns their light on.

If someone is in a negative mood, like dominoes, everyone's energy around that person starts tumbling south. The same goes for sending out good energy and light. We humans are like beads in a necklace. We affect one another. We are connected to one another. We influence one another. And it's time we notice and use this information to our advantage. Charlie, my teacher, taught me that turning on your bright light is our basic purpose in life.

Do you ever consciously turn on your light? If you're not in the habit of this, or if it hasn't occurred to you, try it. See what happens. Give it a chance. Try turning on your light in easy places, like in the coffee shop, and in difficult places, like in a heated argument with a family member. Take charge of your light, turning it on in dark rooms, dark energy fields. Turn on your light and see who notices. Don't be surprised if everybody looks up and smiles. Have you ever heard the expression, "All the world loves a lover"? A lover is a person whose bright light is on high in the world, loving life, loving themselves, loving others. Not from the ego standpoint, but from their joyful, authentic, openhearted spirit. Being that bright light in the world is the secret to real power, because love is powerful. It's powerful because it's infectious with everyone around you. It brings encouragement, optimism, hope, laughter, all the things that bring you back to the fifth dimension and to the truth of who you are.

You know what else is interesting about being a light in the world? You are immediately relieved of the heavy burden of overthinking. You ever notice how overthinking is a drag, overthinking is draining, and it sucks the joy out of you? Of course you need to use your thinking abilities to execute tasks, but to sit and think yourself to death instead of creating sucks the life right out of you. Being a bright light in the world counters this kind of futile, draining exercise.

The kind that is really just worry: "How am I going to do that? What would allow that today? How can I even fake it till I make it? How can I experiment so I get a direct result?" Soul mastery is recognizing that you are here to shine your bright light in the world. If it's that simple, ultimately, then of course you can do it. Especially when you know you are not alone. This is the divine law.

LESSON 22

THE NEW YOU

Dear one, you are returning to your true nature. It is happening with and without your conscious commitment. Everyone who is in the Earth's plane at this time committed to being in body is in the process of returning to their original and true frequency of unconditional love. Our prompts, our invitations, our guidance is simply to help you remember who you really and naturally are.

Do not trouble your spirit with worry and concern that you may miss out on or not elevate or acquire the light you need, or that in some way you may fail to return to your true nature. It is not possible. The Emissaries' assistance is simply to make the experience easier, more joyful, more understood to help the part of you, the ego mind, to learn the new ways to support who you really are rather than fight who you really are. That is a profound healing. It is not the ego itself that is the problem. It is the program in that the ego of you has been imposed with that is causing all the pain and difficulty. Your ego is the outer part of your soul. It wants to help the new. You simply provide new instruction to the ego. Your assignment is to support your spirit, to express the truth of who you are.

The assignment of the ego is to be creative and helpful and assist what your inner self is calling for. Not to attack but to ally with your inner self. That is how you make peace with your ego self. It is not at all the problem. The instructions are the problem: the values you've been given, the rules, the impressions you've been told that you are not worthy, that the ego has accepted as truth, that your ego is who you are. Make peace with your egoic self. When it is acting up and it is afraid, simply reassure it: "You have new assignments to support this new me, this bright light that I am, and I'm grateful and love you for this." Then you create peace within.

If you find resistance, reassure that part of you that is scared: "I love you. We are loved. All is well." Seek peace. Seek harmony. Reassure the parts of you that are afraid; rather than reject them, reeducate them with love and humor. Do not be heavy-handed with yourself as those who have gone before you have been heavy-handed with you. There has been enough of this judgment and indictment and threat. We invite you to live your life with love and humor, to embrace all parts of you. To see the egoic part of you as an ally that just requires new and consistent instructions and reassurance. Reward the ego in you when it aligns with your spirit and assists in helping you live your true nature. It's simply a job of asking your ego to say yes: "How can I help with your spirit?" rather than "How dare you think that I have to stop you?"

We are helping. The universe is so populated with love pouring onto this planet that no one will be left behind, not even you. Everyone who chooses to stay in the physical body is committed to growth and to acquire soul mastery. The Earth itself is a living being that will support you. Spirit helpers are available. Look around. Notice how all of life is working very hard to bring you back to the light of who you are. Change the focus of the ego off the darkness of the world, and turn on the light of your spirit; encourage your ego to see, celebrate, and be in this light, to bask in this light, to relax in this light.

While it may appear that everything is in chaos at the moment, what is falling apart is giving way to a gorgeous new Earth. Be part of that new Earth by committing to reconnecting with your spirit and living the spirit of you instead of the fear of you. Judge *nothing, even you. Be neutral. Be available. Be loving. Be confident. Relax. Whatever you need in the physical plane, whatever level of abundance, relax—we will provide. Allow yourself to receive. Allow yourself to follow the guidance that will connect you with source and flow. Allow yourself to change your mind and reorient your attention so that health and vitality, love, and connection become your new normal. Relax, breathe, and allow yourself to be healed, to be made whole. This is not an invitation to be passive and do nothing. It is an invitation to stop fighting who you really are, doubting the truth that you feel and sense in your heart and bones. Stop ignoring the direction coming to you from your divine spirit, your higher self, and your support team in spirit. Stop numbing out. Get back into your body and breathe. The breath is the bridge between the physical and the spiritual realm. Please establish that bridge so that you navigate both with grace. Ask for help. Focus on your intentions. Be patient when things are not going your way; simply examine what is unfolding. You are here to learn. You are here to grow, and if there is a challenge, see it as an invitation and opportunity to grow, not as an obstacle or setback. All is well. We are forever at your service, and your spirit is forever present, and your soul is fully committed to growing. Trust this and relax. All is well.*

We are all in his great ascension together. It is a very exciting time. Sometimes I wake up in the morning, and I feel like I've entered some energetic version of Disneyland. There are all kinds of wild rides to be had this day, both those I'm personally on and those that I see others on around me. But let us remember that this whole experience, our whole embodiment, is temporary. It is creation school. We're all learning at our own pace. There is no absolute right and wrong. We're all discovering what feels true and good for me right now. We do affect one another, and we are all given the same opportunity to have a glorious life even though it doesn't appear so in the external world. We can't judge the world by appearances, and we can't react to the world by appearances either. If we keep turning on the bright light, it gets easier.

This brings to mind a client, Sherry, whom I worked with years ago. Sherry won a very large lottery in the United States, and her life went from struggle and poverty, really living paycheck to paycheck and sometimes no paycheck, to an abundance of money that was incomprehensibly big overnight. But did she relax? Did she settle in, or did she resist? Well, I'm sure you can guess that it wasn't an easy process, and truthfully, she never did relax with her bounty. "I didn't feel I deserved this." That is the old rule, suggesting that anything good has to be deserved by a not-very-easily-impressed God who isn't going to give you much, if anything, at all because you have no value. Sherry struggled with that old imprint, then squandered a lot of the money, suffered from people asking for the money, and struggled accepting the money left with grace. She got better, but by then, most of the money was gone. Sherry didn't care. In the end, she'd had enough fun with it and enough trouble and found peace.

Respecting the divine laws in this transmission will bring you peace. They exist to create a peaceful life you love. If you are consistent, committed, have an open heart, are willing to be responsible, and are open to life being easier, if you release your fears and anxieties and do what you love as much as you can, you'll win the lottery of a sort too. A lasting drama-free lottery. You'll be happy.

We are all being invited to live in a higher way. This decision is ultimately one we each make individually. Will you agree and then practice living in a higher way, or will you fight it? That's a question we must all answer right now.

If you are here, you have answered. You are ready. Beyond these instructions and guidance is a vote of confidence and a transmission of love from Joachim and the Emissaries of the Third Ray of Love that you've got this, you are going to succeed, you are transforming, and you are now part of the new Earth. You are getting better and better at navigating in this new frequency, and you might feel shaky at times, but you've got this. I want to leave you with that message. You are returning to your true nature, your heart is opening, your vibration is elevating, your intuition is working, your power is rising, and your joy is being restored. On a personal level, thank you so much for being part of this transmission. I've learned and have refreshed a lot myself, and I want you to know we're all in this together. It's important to know that you belong. You're part of this. No matter what your ego says, it's never about being good enough. It's about allowing yourself to be the most expansive beautiful frequency of love that you are. This is the divine law.

Enjoy Being in Creation School, Reflecting on the Invitations and the Encouragement to the New You

Perhaps some of these lessons you've already learned. If you do meet life with grace, for example, and you're not just fighting everyone or everything, then you are mastering this lesson. But if you find you're reactive and triggered, well, you're a student. So, if you are a student of this law, no problem. Simply practice going back to your body and breathing self-love. Some days you'll be better at meeting life with grace than others. No worries. Notice what triggers you and ask for divine help with this so you stay neutral, meet the challenge with grace, and remain peaceful. If you are easily annoyed, realize you are a student and ask yourself, "What am I doing or not doing for myself that makes me so irritable, that makes me so impatient?" The more you learn to stay calm when it's challenging, the sooner you move into the phase of the apprentice, then the journeyman.

If you committed to being graceful, you are on your way to mastery. If the vibe doesn't feel right and you are stuck and your clay feet can't move, then you are a student. So, pay attention to the discomfort and the consequences of being stuck and the toll it's especially taking on your body. Consider this: Actually start moving your feet. Do a little dancing. If you find, "Well, at least I know I should move along, and I am listening to my spirit; I'm just not quite there," then you're an apprentice. So, look for examples of other people who have moved along that'll give you encouragement. We are all connected. Keep the dance going, and if you are someone who just cannot abide by being in something incongruent, well, you're certainly a journeyman. You may well be on your way to mastery, and as you move into mastery, do know that your example becomes the teacher to others. You're helping fulfill your purpose.

The big opportunity right now is to follow inner guidance and not outer noise, because with technology, outer noise is blaring at us on social media 24/7, with nonstop news channels. It's too much. We're not designed to be absorbing all this input, so if you're completely mesmerized by all of this, you're a student; shut it down. Put yourself on a schedule. Limit your input from the outer world and the outer noise, and if you're really depressed by what the outer world is reflecting, that really tells you it's time to shut it down. If you're starting to question what the outer noise is saying—"Hey, wait a minute; it isn't all that bad. I'm not going to believe what I'm being told"—great, you're now a student. You get to decide, "If I am going to listen, what am I listening to? I'm going to be discerning, selective, but ultimately still go back to my spirit."

And the same with, "Listen. I've shut it all down. I am done with that." You are well into journeyman, on to mastery, and the more you shut down the outer noise and listen to your nurse spirit, the more you're the teacher. You are the inspiration. This is how it works. Now, the big one that I find most people resisting is committing to healing what blocks you and, again, getting the therapy you need. Do the self-reflection. Find the support groups, but beyond that, also start allowing yourself to do what your spirit is telling you to do. Please let me paint. Please let me write. Please let me dance. Please let me get on my bike and go play without a guilt trip.

Let yourself live joyfully. Most of us are still in the student or apprentice phase, but if you are so fortunate to have come back to that awareness to live joyfully, please turn it on big time, because your joyful vibes will help others in a big way. We are here for one purpose: to intentionally create a life we love. If you are doing that, thank you. You're helping us all. If you're moving in that direction, thank you. You're helping us all carry on and find examples and follow them. If you're really stuck in a life you hate, okay, observe and don't forget: You have a choice. So start finding and journaling and looking for ways to do something you love, because one step, one hour at a time, you'll start creating the life you love.

Don't be afraid; don't be frustrated. Don't judge yourself. The fact you're even reading this shows you're ready to move back into your true nature and learn to master this. You can be a bright light the minute you decide. All you have to do is smile; it pulls back the curtains of your heart and lets that light shine through. That light makes this the power that your heart has to beat. That light is your spirit, so practice smiling.

Now, I laugh because there's this statement that goes around, especially for women, although I don't think it's particular to women, of what we call resting bitch face, which is just a scowl and a frown and something negative, and it really doesn't project a very good vibe into the world. You may have it and not notice it, so pull the corners of your mouth up to your ears, smile, breathe in, and let out a deep sigh.

Ah, there you go. You in this moment are being a bright light in the world. Keep doing that. Keep practicing. Keep noticing who is and keep mirroring that, and you will soon master that. In other words, this entire process is something that's naturally happening to all of us. The soul mastery lessons that the Emissaries have brought forward are to just make the whole experience enjoyable, to move us out of fear and panic and move us into creativity, curiosity, and joy. I do absolutely want to reiterate along with the Emissaries, you do have this. You will succeed. You are evolving; it is happening. You won't mess up. Be patient. Be relaxed but intentional. If you're patient, relaxed, and intentional, before you know it, you'll be in the frequency and mastering the frequency of your divine self. We're in this together. Thank you for your light. Thank you for sharing time with me as we share the light of the Emissaries, and let's all go forward with an optimistic, encouraged heart and a lot of love. All my love.

A Word on My Teachers

Throughout my entire life, I have been told, "You're so lucky that you're so intuitive. I really want to be intuitive like you are and trust my vibes like you do. I want to fearlessly live my spirit and joyfully trust that my life is unfolding in perfect order, because I see you do." When I hear this, I can't help but acknowledge that I am indeed very lucky to have such a strong connection to spirit and a clear and grounded sense of purpose, as well as an unshakable confidence in the partnership I have with the universe. But I'm not randomly lucky, nor would I actually say that I am lucky at all. Rather, what appears to be "luck" from the outside world's perspective is actually the consequence of having been trained from an early age by fantastic, masterful teachers who empowered me to live in the higher dimensions. It is this very gift of having been taught to be awakened, intuitive, and empowered that has driven my devotion and purpose to continue teaching in the same spirit of love, integrity, and devotion to the empowerment of others that I received. Their work lives on through mine, and I thank them with all my heart and spirit for allowing me to continue to pass this light on.

Let me share here a little more about these incredible teachers in my life. The first of these was my mother, Sonia Choquette, after whom I was named. A lot of people assume I had a classic nurturing mother who baked cookies and did laundry and kept us safe and sound, but she was not at all like that. My mother was like a wild stallion. We cooked for her. We did the laundry and made sure all was in order for her. She was off creating or talking to angels and spirit guides and making fabulous art. So, in terms of classic mothering, that is not what I received from her. What I did get from her was a spiritual teacher who let me know the sky was the limit when it came to possibility if I only imagined it; who made me aware I was a beautiful spirit; and who taught me to never question my worth, to live free of approval, to always trust my vibes, and to live fearlessly, authentically, courageously, and never give my power away.

I learned by watching her live this way as much as from anything or anyone else. I learned from how she related to me and my siblings growing up. If I would ask my mom's permission for something, for example, before she'd answer she would very spontaneously ask, "What does your spirit say?" then, "Do that." It was unorthodox, and she gave me a lot of responsibility at a very young age. There were many times I wished I had baked cookies waiting for me, but what I did receive was the gift of having an accurate mirroring of who I am and all limitations removed from my path. She was not trapped by the control of the outer world due to the circumstances that brought her to America and made her my mom. She lost her family when she was a child during the war. When she was a prisoner in a war camp, she lost her hearing due to rheumatic fever, and she didn't go to school past age 12. So my mom did not get schooled in cultural control. She lived outside the lines of traditional influences, in a world of creativity, art, and spirit. A joyful world. To connect with my mom, rather than her coming into the third dimension to meet me (or her other kids, or anyone for that matter), we had to go into her fourth- and fifth-dimension worlds, which were endlessly beautiful. She used to say, "There's never a problem, only a failure of imagination, and there's always a solution. It's our game of life to find it."

She taught herself photography and took it to a masterful level. She was also a master seamstress and interior designer. Most of all, she was a talented, intuitive guide. She did everything she was interested in and wanted to do. Nothing intimidated her, including not knowing how to do something. "I'll learn as I go," being forever the journeyman in life. She'd ask, "How hard can it be?" Then she learned how hard it was and still succeeded, over and over again. My mom didn't care for cooking. We made dinner, and it was all pretty yucky. But we had a life of spirit, fun, dance, creativity, and endless imagination, so I have no complaints. We were taught to please our spirits, not outside authorities. We were never encouraged to ask permission; she said, "If your spirit tells you to do something, do it. Just be willing to live with your choice." She was my first and most fun teacher.

My next major teacher was Charlie Goodman, whom I met through my mom when I was 12 years old. He was a retired engineer by profession and a master theosophist and intuitive reader by spiritual training. Charlie taught me the intuitive skills of clairvoyance, clairaudience, clairsentience, and trance channeling, as well as how to do intuitive readings, how to work with oracles, how to meditate, how to establish energetic boundaries, and how to be discerning with spirit guides and the different types of spirit guides.

Charlie gave me an in-depth understanding and a profound interactive tour of the subtle spirit realms and taught me how to communicate with the subtle realms at the highest level. Charlie held me to high standards as a student as well. My training was rigorous and thorough but filled with love and laughter. We arranged to meet every Friday night at 7 P.M., which, for a young teenager, which I was, was challenging in itself, because that was when all the fun stuff, such as school sports events, were scheduled. This was my first test of commitment. I had a calling even then, so this wasn't going to stop me. However, one time, in the first few weeks of working with him, I showed up just a few minutes late. When I rang the bell, Charlie didn't answer, which was so confusing for me. I wondered if he was hard of hearing and didn't hear the bell. Then I worried that he was senile and had forgotten about our class. When he still didn't answer after 30 minutes, I feared he dropped dead and that was why he didn't come to the door. It never occurred to me that my being late was the reason. There were no cell phones at that time, so I had to use a landline to call and find out what happened to him. I called and called all week, and still, he didn't answer. When I returned the next week, on time, he opened the door and smiled. My first reaction was to scream, "Charlie, where were you last week? I thought you were dead." He laughed and he said, "Where was I? Where were you? I was here. The spirit guides were here. Your teacher guides were here, but you were nowhere to be found, so we left." From that 12-year-old moment on, I realized if I wanted to live a spirit-guided life, I had to show up on time. I had to make it my priority. I had to be disciplined and responsible and keep my word and commitments. I couldn't fit my classes in when I wanted to or be casual or late. I attribute that particular lesson to the success of my life more than anything else. I learned to honor my word and show up on time. I learned to be clear and reliable. Those became my core values. The universe showed up for me with the same consistency I showed up with.

My third most influential teacher was Dr. Trenton Tully, who founded the Metaphysical Research Society in Denver and who taught me the metaphysical laws of the universe. I studied with him for years at the same time I studied with Charlie. Dr. Tully taught his students that all suffering was the result of not applying what we know about using our consciousness to better our life and that of the world. He was the one who taught me the power of decision, and how to stop playing the game of "I have no choice" that dominates the third dimension. "Everything is a choice," he reminded us, "and we cannot escape the consequences of any choice we make." From Dr. Tully I learned about the evolution of the soul and how to create our own reality. It was mind-blowing to learn something so life altering and empowering at only 15 years old. From him I learned how our consciousness is the architect of our experience, and life doesn't "happen" to anyone. We choose our life. I also learned the need for taking spiritual responsibility for my life from Dr. Tully, and how responsibility is essential to our success. If my life was not working, I was solely responsible for making it better. No one else. The buck stopped with me. My training with Dr. Tully gave me the keys to the kingdom of personal power. Because of my training with him, I was able to direct my life in a way that supported my values and purpose, and never felt controlled by outer conditions or people. I had to pay attention, be present, control my thoughts and emotions, and be responsible for the gift of my life. The best followed. Dr. Tully taught me the universe was my partner, and life is not a random, chaotic journey I had to navigate on my own. I also learned that my highest purpose was to serve humanity, teach what I had learned, and be an unwavering light of love in the world.

Acting on what I knew in my heart even then, that teaching was my purpose, I jumped in and taught my first class when I was around 15 or 16. I had three students. The first was a woman that I had done intuitive readings for over the years. In fact, she was the one who asked me to teach her everything I knew, and I agreed. The second was her brother, a truck driver who came to Denver every other week on his route, and the third was his out-of-town mistress. I was so young and naive at the time, I didn't even know or care what a mistress was. I was just happy to have students. Acting on pure faith, I taught them for the next six weeks a class on how to do intuitive readings, and I loved every minute. It was so rewarding and successful, I never looked back. I have devoted my life to empowering others with their intuitive faculties ever since. My purpose was clear from that class forward.

Each of my three teachers gave me an invaluable gift. My mom gave me the gift of imagination. Hers was unlimited, setting the stage for expanding my own. She also taught me that I was a deeply loved divine being, giving me the confidence to trust myself and take risks in life. Charlie taught me the psychic arts, how to do intuitive readings, and how to navigate the subtle realms with masterful skill. And Dr. Tully taught me the laws of the universe, how not to be a victim, how to be an empowered and masterful creator, and how to be of service.

My newest teachers, the Emissaries, who appear throughout this transmission, arrived in 2002 and are major teachers in my life and for others. They came to help us navigate this Earth transition period we are now in, and I'm hugely grateful for their reassuring direction. I know we're all here at this time to grow, to bring in the new Earth. And though it looks like all chaos is breaking loose, with the Emissaries' help, we will rise to highest frequencies and be free of this chaos unfolding now.

I'd like to leave you with this message from them all. Trust yourself. Trust the spirit in you. Trust the spirit, and look for the spirit in others. Look for the spirit and live in joy.

They all hope, as I do, that you enjoyed this transmission.

All my love,

SONIA

ABOUT THE AUTHOR

SONIA CHOQUETTE is celebrated worldwide as an author, spiritual teacher, six-sensory consultant, and transformational visionary guide. Sonia's expertise is sought throughout the world, helping both individuals and organizations dramatically improve their experience and abilities to perform at optimal levels through empowerment and transformation. Sonia attended the University of Denver and the Sorbonne in Paris. Sonia now resides in Paris.
Website: **soniachoquette.net**

Hay House Titles of Related Interest

YOU CAN HEAL YOUR LIFE, the movie,
starring Louise Hay & Friends
(available as an online streaming video)
www.hayhouse.co.uk/louise-movie

THE SHIFT, the movie,
starring Dr Wayne W. Dyer
(available as an online streaming video)
www.hayhouse.co.uk/the-shift-movie

***

ANGELS ARE WITH YOU NOW, by Kyle Gray

A BEGINNER'S GUIDE TO THE UNIVERSE: Uncommon Ideas for Living an Unusually Happy Life, by Mike Dooley

MAKING THE AFTERLIFE CONNECTION: The Journey from Doubt to Knowing That Death Is Not the End, by Suzanne Giesemann

THE 15 SUCCESS PRINCIPLES FOR SELF-REALIZATION: Channelled Wisdom to Create Your Reality and Expand Your Perspective, by Sara Landon

All of the above are available at your local bookstore,
or may be ordered by contacting Hay House (see next page).

***

We hope you enjoyed this Hay House book. If you'd like to receive our online catalogue featuring additional information on Hay House books and products, please contact:

Hay House UK Ltd
1st Floor, Crawford Corner,
91–93 Baker Street, London W1U 6QQ
Tel: +44 (0)20 3927 7290; www.hayhouse.co.uk

Published in the United States of America by:
Hay House LLC
PO Box 5100, Carlsbad, CA 92018-5100
Tel: (760) 431-7695 or (800) 654-5126
www.hayhouse.com

Published in Australia by:
Hay House Australia Publishing Pty Ltd
18/36 Ralph St., Alexandria NSW 2015
Tel: +61 (02) 9669 4299
www.hayhouse.com.au

Published in India by:
Hay House Publishers (India) Pvt Ltd
Muskaan Complex, Plot No. 3,
B-2, Vasant Kunj, New Delhi 110 070
Tel: +91 11 41761620
www.hayhouse.co.in

Let Your Soul Grow
Experience life-changing transformation – one video at a time – with guidance from the world's leading experts.
www.healyourlifeplus.com

TRANSFORM YOUR DAY— ANYTIME, ANYWHERE

With the **Empower You** Unlimited Audio *App*

66 ☆☆☆☆☆ **Life changing.**
My fav app on my entire phone, hands down! – Gigi 99

Unlimited access to the entire Hay House audio library!

You'll get:

- 600+ soul-stirring **audiobooks** to expand your mind
- 1,000+ **meditations** for restful sleep, morning focus, and gentle healing
- Bite-sized audios **under 20 minutes**—perfect for busy days
- **Exclusive talks** you won't find anywhere else
- **Daily affirmations**
- Fresh content added **every week** to fuel your journey

New audios added every week!

66 Driving, yard work, and housework have been **transformed**! – Ruffles27 99

Scan the QR code to start listening or visit **hayhouse.com/unlimited**

CONNECT WITH
HAY HOUSE
ONLINE

🌐 hayhouse.co.uk   **f** @hayhouse

📷 @hayhouseuk   🦋 @hayhouseuk.bsky.social

🎵 @hayhouseuk   ▶ @HayHousePresents

Find out all about our latest books & card decks • Be the first to know about exclusive discounts • Interact with our authors in live broadcasts • Celebrate the cycle of the seasons with us • Watch free videos from your favourite authors • Connect with like-minded souls

'The gateways to wisdom and knowledge are always open.'

Louise Hay